The IDEA Book

Improvement through TEI
(Total Employee Involvement)

Edited by
Japan Human Relations Association

Foreword by Norman Bodek
President
Productivity, Inc.

Introduction by Kenjiro Yamada
Managing Director
Japan Human Relations Association

Productivity Press
CAMBRIDGE, MASSACHUSETTS
NORWALK, CONNECTICUT

The IDEA Book

Improvement through TEI
(Total Employee Involvement)

Originally published as *Kaizen teian handobukku*, copyright © 1980 by Japan Human Relations Association. Translated into English by Productivity, Inc.

English translation copyright © 1988 by Productivity, Inc.

Productivity Press   Productivity, Inc.
P.O. Box 3007   or   101 Merritt 7 Corporate Park
Cambridge, MA 02140   5th Floor
(617) 497-5146   Norwalk, CT 06851
                                                       (203) 846-3777

Library of Congress Catalog Card Number: 85-63498
ISBN: 0-915299-22-4

Book and cover design by Joyce C. Weston
Typeset by Rudra Press, Cambridge, MA
Printed and bound by The Maple-Vail Book Manufacturing Group
Printed in the United States of America

Library of Congress Cataloging-in-Publication Data

Kaizen teian handobukku.   English.
   The idea book.

   Translation of: *Kaizen teian handobukku.*
   Includes index.
   1. Works councils — Japan.   2. Industrial management — Japan — Employee participation.   I. Nihon H R Kyōkai.
HD5660.J3K3513   1988   658.3'152   88-42627
ISBN 0-915299-22-4

89 90 10 9 8 7 6 5 4 3 2

Contents

Publisher's Foreword

Our company conducts frequent study missions to Japan. On them I often stop and ask workers to tell me about their most recent ideas:

> "I used to have to bend over deeply to push these two buttons that activate the punch press. My idea was to move the buttons higher so I wouldn't have to bend."

> "This tray would slide down the ramp, hit the end, and occasionally a part would bounce out. Now the small metal bar I installed prevents that from happening."

> "In the past it was necessary for two people to hold a board while it was cut at this machine. My idea was to build an extension to the machine to hold the board. Now I can cut the board without anyone else's help."

> "I would sometimes produce a defect when I moved the grinding wheel too far forward. I devised this metal restraining bar to prevent that from happening."

In nearly every plant we visit in Japan, employees have similar things to tell about — ideas they have thought up and implemented to improve their work, their products, their company, and their own lives on the job.

I am sincerely pleased that you are reading *The Idea Book*. This is one of the most important books we are publishing this year, because it is the first book in English that tells how to successfully set up and participate in a Japanese-style suggestion system, the cornerstone of a company plan for Total Employee Involvement (TEI).

Total Employee Involvement is an American system incorporating a number of revolutionary Japanese techniques for awakening the creative resources of workers to improve the product, the job, the workers' lives, and the company as a whole. The result of a carefully developed TEI program is a strong, competitive company unified by every employee's sense of participation in the corporate "family" and by mutual trust and respect between workers and management. There are many good examples in Japan and a growing number in the United States (such as

NUMMI, the joint venture between Toyota and General Motors in Fremont, California).

The various aspects of a Total Employee Involvement program are discussed in depth in Productivity's *TEI Newsletter* and taught by experienced managers and trainers at our TEI conferences. The most important component, however, is the vital, total-participation suggestion system that you are about to discover in this handbook.

In Japan, suggestion systems are part of ongoing daily company improvement efforts known as *kaizen*. Unlike a typical American suggestion system that seeks and accepts only a few good ideas and is relatively slow to respond to proposals, the Japanese-style system encourages all workers to continually re-examine their jobs and their products to think about how things could be improved. The proposals are reviewed by a committee that gives feedback within days rather than weeks, and workers receive money awards for their implemented ideas (many systems also give a small reward for each suggestion submitted).

This type of high-participation system produces a phenomenal number of ideas per year. In 1986, Japanese companies received nearly 48 million ideas from their employees. While U.S. employees submitted over 1 million ideas to their companies, Toyota alone received *2.65 million* suggestions from its employees — and spent several million dollars to reward them for their ideas.

As Kenjiro Yamada points out, however, workers participate in the suggestion system not just for the money prizes but for the satisfaction of continually using their minds and creativity to improve their workplace and the goods or services they produce. In the view of Mr. Yamada, managing director of the Japan Human Relations Association (the national association for corporate improvement programs), participative suggestion systems definitely produce financial benefits and make companies more competitive, but the primary benefit is the development of employees' morale and self-respect through opportunities for creative expression and recognition. When you as a worker know that your ideas matter to management and you genuinely feel you are part of a team that takes your interest into account, your company becomes stronger, more responsive to internal and external challenges, and more competitive. A company that brings in 100 ideas from each employee each year can't help but have an edge over a company that is lucky to average one suggestion per worker. Everyone benefits from this strengthening.

This book is particularly wonderful because it's written for workers to use. It doesn't just say "this is how they do it in Japan and you should try to copy it." Although acceptance of the Japanese *model* — management commitment and involvement, a reward system, and timely response — is treated as a given and should be taken seriously by all American managers, the primary function of *The Idea Book* is a hands-on teaching tool for workers and supervisors to refer to again and again. It gives hundreds of examples and checklists for things like how to look for problems in the workplace, how to use simple graphic techniques to record data, how to write and illustrate suggestions for better evaluation, and how to solve problems by working together in small groups. This is a very accessible book, flavored with illustrations, examples, and personal statements from employees who have participated in suggestion and improvement programs in Japan.

Many of the workers quoted in *The Idea Book* talk about their own transformations through the process of making suggestions. Not everyone warmed to it instantly. But it's wonderfully inspiring to read how an uninterested worker at a job he thought was boring was able to become a happier, more creative, more enthusiastic participant in an environment with infinite possibilities for improvement. It can happen anywhere, and with the help of this book, I hope it will happen at your company soon.

I would like to thank Karen Jones and Reiko Kano for their work editing the English version of *The Idea Book*; Esmé McTighe for supervising production; Joyce Weston for the book and cover design; Marie A. Kascus for the index; and Caroline Kutil, Michele Seery, and Susan Cobb of Rudra Press for typesetting and layout.

Norman Bodek
President
Productivity, Inc.

Introduction

As the saying "work smarter, not harder" implies, the suggestion system — an important vehicle for employee creativity and independent initiative — has become a key activity on many shop floors in Japan.

The Japanese-style suggestion system, or *teian*, is a practical aspect of *kaizen*, the process of continual improvement involving every employee. Workers participate in the suggestion system not only for the money awards that are standard in most Japanese systems, but for the satisfaction of using their minds and creativity every day to improve the place where they work and the goods or services they produce. The suggestion system, first and foremost, builds the workers' morale and self-respect. It shows them they are important members of the company family, with ideas that count. The company benefits from the worker's participation as well as from the aggregate financial benefits of the ideas they produce.

Although company suggestion systems were originally brought to Japan from the West after World War II, teian has developed into a process quite distinct from the typical American system. Rather than striving for a small number of "champions" to come up with a few big ideas for saving the company a lot of money, the Japanese-style system encourages all employees to continually think of ideas, no matter how small, for improving any aspect of their jobs, not just cost. Ideas are evaluated quickly and a reward system based on the quality of the ideas provides additional incentive.

Developing such a "living" suggestion system in the workplace takes more than announcing the program and setting up a suggestion box. To enjoy the continued, full, and active participation of all workers requires tireless dedication from the suggestion system coordinators and work supervisors who must maintain the proper environment. This handbook is designed to help these leaders and their workers learn to spot problems for improvement, make better written suggestions, and work together in small groups to tackle bigger problems and develop more comprehensive solutions.

The absence of small group activities in the workplace is a common reason for a suggestion system just not getting off the ground. Although making improvement suggestions is in some ways very individual-oriented, by sharing ideas with other group members, employees can refine their suggestions and come up with better solutions to the problems discovered in the workplace. The voluntary small group activities of Japanese-style suggestion systems are a major factor in their success.

In introducing a suggestion system in the workplace, do not place too much emphasis on the word "suggestion." Many workers hear this word and immediately conclude that the program is too difficult or time-consuming or that they do not know anything to suggest. We hope that this handbook will help suggestion system coordinators and floor supervisors respond to these concerns and answer frequently asked questions.

An issue that frequently arises in the early stages of a suggestion system is whether to stress quality or quantity. In my opinion it is better to start with quantity. Workers cannot propose great qualitative improvements until they become so familiar with the suggestion system that it becomes part of their work life. The leaders must be able to recognize when the system has matured to the point where the emphasis can be shifted to quality.

A Japanese-style suggestion system develops in three stages. In Stage I (typically one to three years), participation and involvement are stressed. Management's primary effort is to encourage all workers to examine their jobs and work areas and think of ways to improve them. Stage II (lasting two to three years) involves development and education of the workers to make them better equipped to analyze problems and devise the best solutions. Concern for the quality of suggestions is introduced during this period. But not until Stage III (usually about five years after the program begins) should management focus its attention on the economic impact of suggestions.

Because a suggestion system deals with real problems, workers need real and illustrative examples to help them. Such examples make up a major portion of this handbook. Regardless of the type of business or industry, actual examples provide the best way to learn the skill of spotting potential improvements. Nothing will please the editors more than knowing this handbook is contributing to improvement in the workplace.

The editors express their deepest appreciation to the suggestion program promotion offices and the office staff of Toyota Motor, Matsushita Electric, Nisshin Steel, Aisin Seiki, Mitsubishi Jiko, and other companies for providing examples of suggestions and personal experiences based on suggestion systems in actual use.

Kenjiro Yamada
Managing Director
Japan Human Relations Association

CHAPTER 1

The Joy of Creation and Invention

The Unique Human Being
Why We Make Suggestions
What a Suggestion System Can Do
Benefits of the Suggestion System:
    Personal Experiences

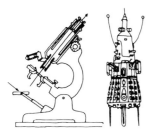

The Unique Human Being

If people did not think, we would not be much different from dogs, cats, rats, and other animals. In fact, lacking the sharp fangs of dogs, the agility of cats, or the environmental adaptability of rats, we are generally weaker and more vulnerable than animals. The wonder of humanness lies in the ability to think.

Through thinking, humans have learned to control nature and make life more convenient and rewarding. Most of us learned in school who invented the conveniences that surround us — the light bulb, telephone, printing press, automobile, steam engine, and so on. But what about the inventors of the tools you are using now — for example, the pen or pencil in your hand? Can you name the inventor of a piece of office equipment, or a shop machine, or a hand tool and its components? How about the inventors of desks, chairs, blackboards, coffee cups, plates, shoes, or clothing? Nobody knows them.

At work and at home we are surrounded by products whose inventors we don't know. Each product, nevertheless, is the embodiment of human creativity and improvements on prior ideas. Every invention reflects human history — the story of ordinary people applying their creative drive to the pursuit of convenience, ease, and a higher quality of life. Civilization rests on such past achievements and the unique adaptability that has enabled humans to survive and thrive on the earth.

Why We Make Suggestions

Instead of asking, "Why do we make suggestions?" we might ask, "What makes us express our creativity? Why are we always looking for ways to improve things?" The answer is obvious. It is human nature to use our creativity to make things better and easier.

Of course, it is important for any organization that its members adhere to established standards and do their work properly. However, if we followed the rules blindly without making any creative contribution, we would be no different from machines and robots.

History of Ideas

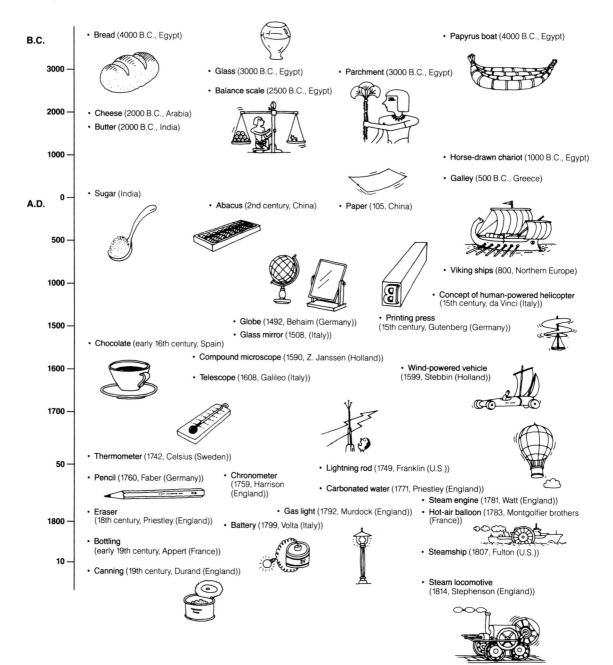

B.C.

- Bread (4000 B.C., Egypt)
- Papyrus boat (4000 B.C., Egypt)

3000

- Glass (3000 B.C., Egypt)
- Parchment (3000 B.C., Egypt)
- Balance scale (2500 B.C., Egypt)

2000

- Cheese (2000 B.C., Arabia)
- Butter (2000 B.C., India)

1000

- Horse-drawn chariot (1000 B.C., Egypt)
- Galley (500 B.C., Greece)

A.D. 0

- Sugar (India)
- Abacus (2nd century, China)
- Paper (105, China)

500

1000

- Viking ships (800, Northern Europe)
- Concept of human-powered helicopter (15th century, da Vinci (Italy))

1500

- Globe (1492, Behaim (Germany))
- Glass mirror (1508, (Italy))
- Printing press (15th century, Gutenberg (Germany))
- Chocolate (early 16th century, Spain)
- Compound microscope (1590, Z. Janssen (Holland))
- Wind-powered vehicle (1599, Stebbin (Holland))

1600

- Telescope (1608, Galileo (Italy))

1700

- Thermometer (1742, Celsius (Sweden))

50

- Lightning rod (1749, Franklin (U.S.))
- Pencil (1760, Faber (Germany))
- Chronometer (1759, Harrison (England))
- Carbonated water (1771, Priestley (England))
- Steam engine (1781, Watt (England))
- Eraser (18th century, Priestley (England))
- Gas light (1792, Murdock (England))
- Hot-air balloon (1783, Montgolfier brothers (France))

1800

- Bottling (early 19th century, Appert (France))
- Battery (1799, Volta (Italy))
- Steamship (1807, Fulton (U.S.))

10

- Canning (19th century, Durand (England))
- Steam locomotive (1814, Stephenson (England))

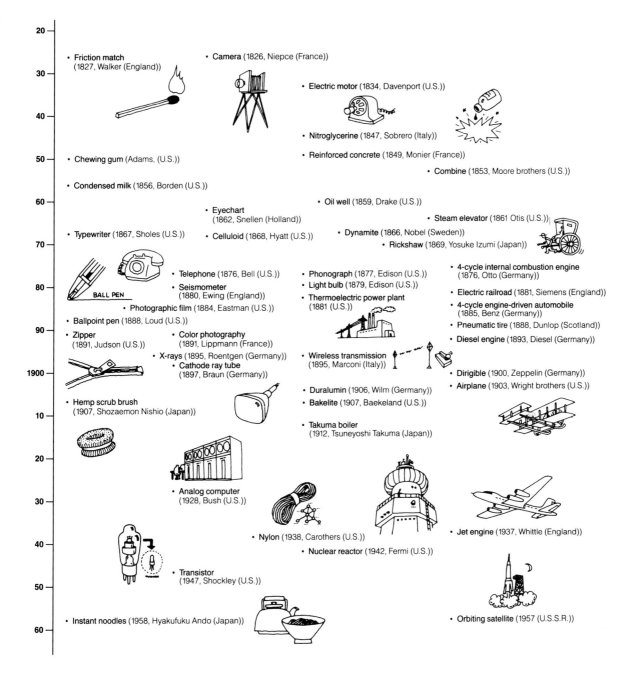

- Friction match (1827, Walker (England))
- Camera (1826, Niepce (France))
- Electric motor (1834, Davenport (U.S.))
- Nitroglycerine (1847, Sobrero (Italy))
- Chewing gum (Adams, (U.S.))
- Reinforced concrete (1849, Monier (France))
- Combine (1853, Moore brothers (U.S.))
- Condensed milk (1856, Borden (U.S.))
- Oil well (1859, Drake (U.S.))
- Eyechart (1862, Snellen (Holland))
- Steam elevator (1861 Otis (U.S.))
- Typewriter (1867, Sholes (U.S.))
- Celluloid (1868, Hyatt (U.S.))
- Dynamite (1866, Nobel (Sweden))
- Rickshaw (1869, Yosuke Izumi (Japan))
- Telephone (1876, Bell (U.S.))
- Phonograph (1877, Edison (U.S.))
- 4-cycle internal combustion engine (1876, Otto (Germany))
- Seismometer (1880, Ewing (England))
- Light bulb (1879, Edison (U.S.))
- Electric railroad (1881, Siemens (England))
- Thermoelectric power plant (1881 (U.S.))
- 4-cycle engine-driven automobile (1885, Benz (Germany))
- Photographic film (1884, Eastman (U.S.))
- Pneumatic tire (1888, Dunlop (Scotland))
- Ballpoint pen (1888, Loud (U.S.))
- Diesel engine (1893, Diesel (Germany))
- Zipper (1891, Judson (U.S.))
- Color photography (1891, Lippmann (France))
- X-rays (1895, Roentgen (Germany))
- Wireless transmission (1895, Marconi (Italy))
- Cathode ray tube (1897, Braun (Germany))
- Dirigible (1900, Zeppelin (Germany))
- Airplane (1903, Wright brothers (U.S.))
- Hemp scrub brush (1907, Shozaemon Nishio (Japan))
- Duralumin (1906, Wilm (Germany))
- Bakelite (1907, Baekeland (U.S.))
- Takuma boiler (1912, Tsuneyoshi Takuma (Japan))
- Analog computer (1928, Bush (U.S.))
- Nylon (1938, Carothers (U.S.))
- Jet engine (1937, Whittle (England))
- Nuclear reactor (1942, Fermi (U.S.))
- Transistor (1947, Shockley (U.S.))
- Instant noodles (1958, Hyakufuku Ando (Japan))
- Orbiting satellite (1957 (U.S.S.R.))

BALL PEN

If a worker only follows orders, he or she is little more than a robot or a part of a machine.

However, a human being senses and thinks while working.

Many ideas occur to us while we work: "This action seems awkward" or "This is wasteful!" or "Our customers would like the product better if we did it this way." These ideas give us important clues to make our work more successful.

The job you are doing now is not perfect. It may involve many inefficiencies. The equipment and machinery, the jigs and fixtures, the office automation systems, and the work standards were probably designed by talented individuals. None of them, however, have direct knowledge of the inconveniences you, the user, experience.

Correcting such deficiencies and inconveniences is up to you. Only you can provide the answer, because the inconveniences you notice are intrinsically your experience.

Improvement is the process through which you develop your own solutions. The *suggestion system* is the process through which your solutions are adopted by management.

Look around you. What you see is the job you must do. You know a lot about the job and its peculiarities. Does the equipment or tool you use have a peculiarity only you know about? Is there an inconvenience that only you know? Is there a method you've always felt should be used?

You can probably answer yes to one of these questions. No matter how trivial it may seem, any change that improves a process or eliminates an inconvenience is welcomed. A greater benefit is achieved when many small problems are solved one by one.

What a Suggestion System Can Do

A suggestion system has a simple basic structure. Each day, as workers find solutions to problems encountered on the job, they write up and present their improvements as suggestions. The suggestions are then evaluated and rewarded on the basis of certain criteria. Details differ between companies, but the underlying character of the suggestion system remains the same.

Suggestions make jobs easier, safer, and more efficient, reduce errors and cost, improve service, and make customers happier. However, it is important to realize that the benefits of a sug-

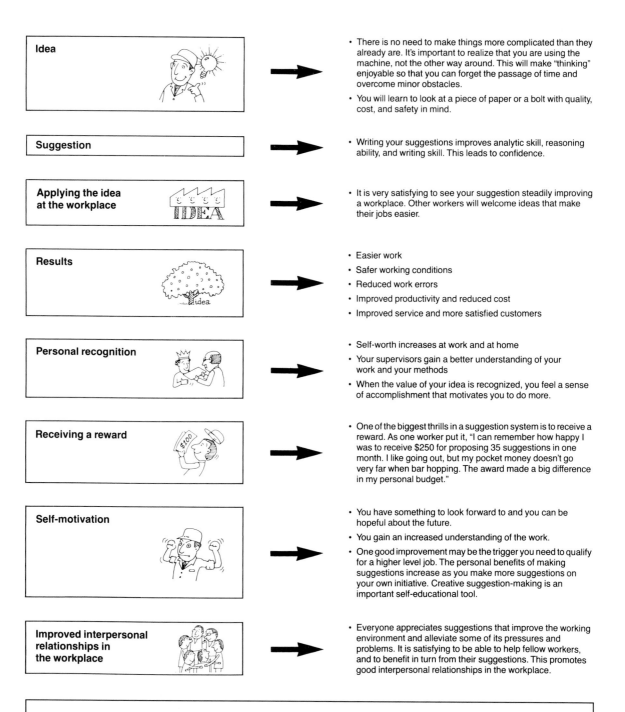

Idea

- There is no need to make things more complicated than they already are. It's important to realize that you are using the machine, not the other way around. This will make "thinking" enjoyable so that you can forget the passage of time and overcome minor obstacles.
- You will learn to look at a piece of paper or a bolt with quality, cost, and safety in mind.

Suggestion

- Writing your suggestions improves analytic skill, reasoning ability, and writing skill. This leads to confidence.

Applying the idea at the workplace

- It is very satisfying to see your suggestion steadily improving a workplace. Other workers will welcome ideas that make their jobs easier.

Results

- Easier work
- Safer working conditions
- Reduced work errors
- Improved productivity and reduced cost
- Improved service and more satisfied customers

Personal recognition

- Self-worth increases at work and at home
- Your supervisors gain a better understanding of your work and your methods
- When the value of your idea is recognized, you feel a sense of accomplishment that motivates you to do more.

Receiving a reward

- One of the biggest thrills in a suggestion system is to receive a reward. As one worker put it, "I can remember how happy I was to receive $250 for proposing 35 suggestions in one month. I like going out, but my pocket money doesn't go very far when bar hopping. The award made a big difference in my personal budget."

Self-motivation

- You have something to look forward to and you can be hopeful about the future.
- You gain an increased understanding of the work.
- One good improvement may be the trigger you need to qualify for a higher level job. The personal benefits of making suggestions increase as you make more suggestions on your own initiative. Creative suggestion-making is an important self-educational tool.

Improved interpersonal relationships in the workplace

- Everyone appreciates suggestions that improve the working environment and alleviate some of its pressures and problems. It is satisfying to be able to help fellow workers, and to benefit in turn from their suggestions. This promotes good interpersonal relationships in the workplace.

The company and the individual workers improve together

gestion system are not limited to improved efficiency and reduced cost. There are substantial personal benefits for the workers.

A suggestion system actively supported by workers revitalizes the workplace. Communication and commitment improve because solving problems and suggesting improvements require a heightened sense of cooperation throughout the company.

Workers increase their understanding about the job as they closely observe the problems around them, and they become more enthusiastic about working as they see their suggestions being adopted on the job. In a very real way, a successful suggestion is a barometer of the morale in the workplace.

How can a suggestion system produce this wide variety of benefits? This book provides some of the answers. But the only way to experience the benefits of a suggestion system is to implement one of your own.

Benefits of the Suggestion System: Personal Experiences

Here are some comments from several workers about what they have gotten from participating in suggestion activities:

☞ *I spent my first days in the company trying to learn my job and become a capable and contributing worker. After I had learned the job pretty well,*

I recommended doing a task in a certain way. My recommendation was accepted and put to immediate use. My superior brought me a suggestion form and urged me to write up my improvement as a suggestion. That was the first time I had seen a suggestion form.

I did not know how to write a suggestion, but I did the best I could. Some time later, I received an envelope with a money reward in it. I can still remember how happy it made me feel.

☞ *My first suggestion was not adopted. However, I remember receiving a small reward and a certificate for my effort and thinking, "Making suggestions isn't all that hard." Since then I have turned in suggestions regularly.*

As I got used to making suggestions, more of them were adopted. This made me more confident and made the job more enjoyable. Regardless of the size of the improvement, knowing that I did something makes me feel very happy.

☞ *I wasn't shooting for high quality when I first started making suggestions. I wasn't even thinking of getting a reward. If you make enough suggestions, though, there's bound to be a few good ones, and I won $45 as a reward. Afterwards, one of my supervisors and several of the engineers came to me with questions.*

That particular supervisor did not usually talk to me. When he came to me to talk, I knew I must have done something pretty important. I realized that my idea had been accepted, and this motivated me to make more suggestions. Now I try my best, and sometimes I make a very good suggestion.

☞ *I made my first suggestion after I had been working at my company for about three years. During one morning meeting, my plant manager passed out some suggestion forms and said: "X received a reward for making a good, creative suggestion. You should try too — you could earn a reward."*

About a month after I made a suggestion, the plant manager came to me and said: "The engineers told me that you made a good suggestion."

I was relieved, because I wasn't sure how good the idea was. Since then, I have continued looking for problems to improve at my workplace and writing suggestions.

I started by writing suggestions to made my work easier. I've won rewards of $15 or $25. Winning a reward makes me feel appreciated and motivates me to write more suggestions. Today, I feel that I am participating in managing my company through the suggestion system.

☞ *Unlike other animals, we can think, look, and listen intelligently. However, when we work on an assembly line at a repetitive task, we begin to feel like we are just part of a machine, and we feel our value as human beings diminish.*

One day, as I was looking at a list of people who made good suggestions, I realized that participating in the suggestion system was the only way I could revive my value as a human being and use my ability to the fullest in the work environment.

So I went to the suggestion office and found out about the proposal system. I set goals and made plans for myself and started my suggestion program.

☞ *I became seriously committed to the suggestion system about ten years ago when my supervisor told me: "I don't care whether it's sports or work. Why don't you become the best in the division at something?" I had just received a $2 reward for a suggestion and I promised myself I would become the best suggester in the division. Since then I have made suggestions like crazy.*

I feel so happy when a suggestion of mine is adopted and someone tells me that it has made his job easier or less physically demanding. Several years after I started making suggestions, I decided I was going to win the gold award. I did my best and won the gold award, which made me number one in the division. I still remember how happy I was. I also remember how good it felt when my supervisor told me my suggestion was saving the company $450 per month. Memories like these keep me motivated to continue making suggestions.

CHAPTER 2

How to Make Improvements

PILING SMALL IMPROVEMENTS
ON TOP OF EACH OTHER

To those who have never made one, a *suggestion* may sound like something very difficult. Many people think they can't do something as difficult as making a suggestion. They may be confusing *suggestions* with *inventions* or thinking of blue-ribbon suggestions they have seen written up in the company newspaper. This is looking at the highest level of creativity, but it is better to set your goals a little lower. Learning to make suggestions is not complicated, and there is no way to reach the top without first mastering some sound fundamentals.

Start with Small Improvements

Start by looking for examples of waste, inconsistency, or inadequacy that are sure to be around you. The important thing is to identify problems close to you and solve these routine problems one by one.

Even people whose suggestions have won company or national-level awards started out by simply eliminating the waste, inefficiency, or inconsistency they saw around them. Steady effort in these areas lays the groundwork necessary for coming up with major improvement suggestions.

Unfortunately, we tend to accept a certain amount of waste as inevitable and ignore what we perceive as trivial problems. If left unchecked and allowed to grow, however, a trivial problem may become major enough to rock the foundation of the company. Given enough time, a leaky faucet can waste enough water drop by drop to fill a lake.

In a company, people, goods, and money are concentrated, and small problems increase geometrically in size. One screw, one piece of paper, five minutes wasted here and there can all add up to significant waste when they are repeated often enough.

Efficiency is achieved when objective and method are balanced. If the method is insufficient for the task, it is inadequate. Waste occurs if the method is excessive for the object. When the method is sometimes wasteful and sometimes inadequate, it is called inconsistent. For example, a one-ton truck should be used for carrying a load of one ton. If you try to use a half-ton truck to carry one ton, the method is inadequate. If you use a two-ton truck, it is wasteful.

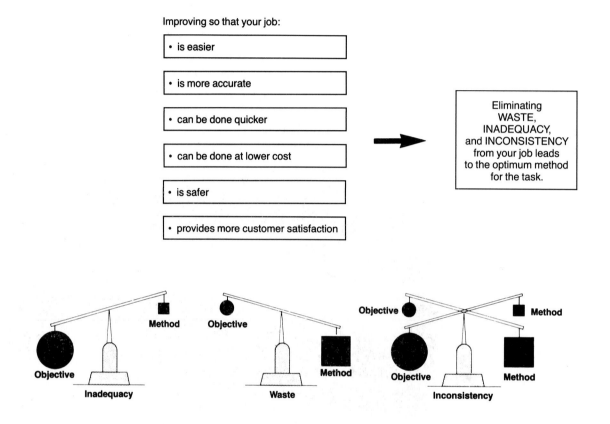

Improving so that your job:

- is easier
- is more accurate
- can be done quicker
- can be done at lower cost
- is safer
- provides more customer satisfaction

Eliminating WASTE, INADEQUACY, and INCONSISTENCY from your job leads to the optimum method for the task.

The job we do every day can be considered a means for accomplishing a certain end. If we evaluate the job in light of the objective and then eliminate waste, inadequacy, and inconsistency, the job will become easier, quicker, safer, cheaper, and more accurate. In other words, efficiency is improved. Look around you. There is waste, inadequacy, and inconsistency everywhere that you can start to reduce.

Improvement Steps

The road to improvement laid by our predecessors, from problem identification, to improvement, and then follow-up, is not a smooth or easy path. Obstacles along the way may be very difficult and may require a lot of trial and error to solve.

The improvement process can be broken down into two stages: *problem identification* and *problem solving*. The problem identification stage has four steps: identification, research, idea formulation, and organization. The problem-solving stage has two steps: improvement implementation and improvement follow-up. These steps apply not only to the suggestion system but to all improvement activities.

Some companies or divisions accept only proposals for improvement, while others accept only suggestions that have actually been implemented. Generally speaking, improvement proposals were the only type of suggestions accepted until the mid-1960s, but starting in the mid-1970s, implemented suggestions began to account for the majority.

Step 1: Problem Identification

"Hmmm, the equipment sounds different today."

"Hmmm, the workpiece doesn't fit well today."

"There're so many errors in this calculation. I wonder what happened."

All problems are deeply rooted in the character of the workplace. The quality of an improvement depends on how deeply you dig to find the root cause. If you immediately jump to a conclusion about the cause, your solution will most likely produce only temporary relief of the symptoms of the problem.

The process of problem identification must be carried out thoroughly so that the real problem is found. Different ideas must be tried until the best solution is obtained.

One definition of a problem is *a deviation from the norm* — the difference between what is expected and what is actually occurring. Reducing or eliminating the difference between the two is solving the problem.

An implication of this definition is that, no matter how long you observe a given phenomenon, a problem does not become apparent unless you know what the ideal, expected state is. In other words, it is impossible to detect a problem unless you know why you are doing the job and what that job's ideal state is.

Improvement Steps

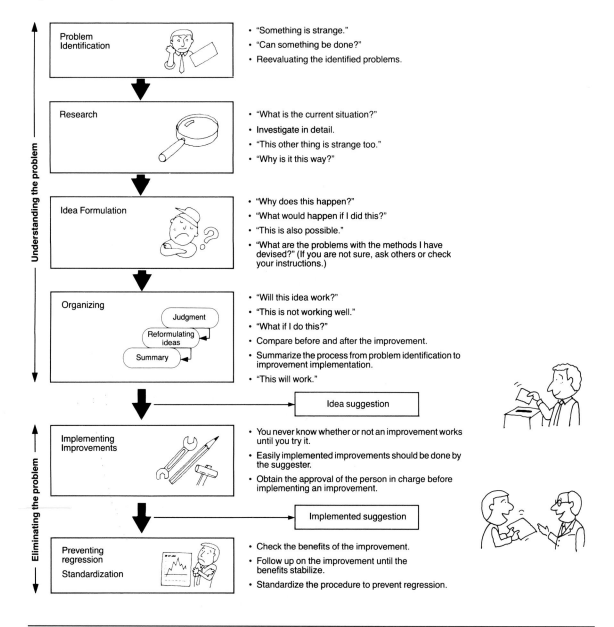

Problem Identification
- "Something is strange."
- "Can something be done?"
- Reevaluating the identified problems.

Research
- "What is the current situation?"
- Investigate in detail.
- "This other thing is strange too."
- "Why is it this way?"

Idea Formulation
- "Why does this happen?"
- "What would happen if I did this?"
- "This is also possible."
- "What are the problems with the methods I have devised?" (If you are not sure, ask others or check your instructions.)

Organizing
- Judgment
- Reformulating ideas
- Summary
- "Will this idea work?"
- "This is not working well."
- "What if I do this?"
- Compare before and after the improvement.
- Summarize the process from problem identification to improvement implementation.
- "This will work."

Idea suggestion

Implementing Improvements
- You never know whether or not an improvement works until you try it.
- Easily implemented improvements should be done by the suggester.
- Obtain the approval of the person in charge before implementing an improvement.

Implemented suggestion

Preventing regression
Standardization
- Check the benefits of the improvement.
- Follow up on the improvement until the benefits stabilize.
- Standardize the procedure to prevent regression.

Understanding the problem

Eliminating the problem

The ABCs of creative suggestion-making:

a. **Think:** Use your mind continuously and improve your thinking power.

b. **Record:** Develop the ability to write and organize your thoughts.

c. **Devise:** Develop and implement the improvements yourself.

d. **Calculate:** Look ahead and become aware of raw cost.

e. **Action:** Be flexible in your action.

All improvements start with the perception of a problem as a slight deviation from the ideal or standard, detected by a sharply honed instinct for catching problems. Most of us encounter numerous slight deviations from established standards during the course of our work each day. In many cases, however, we either ignore these deviations or fix them with makeshift solutions; we don't see them as areas for improvement for the long term.

Most jobs are already fairly well managed. If we do not develop our perception to notice these deviations, we may imagine that there are no problems to be solved. This attitude becomes stronger as familiarity with the job increases, and eventually we can lose all ability to detect deviations from the norm.

You should learn to analyze the workplace carefully in terms of its ideal, most efficient and convenient state. If you look at your workplace with this ideal in mind, you will probably notice mountains of problems. In that sense, the workplace is a source of creativity and inventiveness — a starting place for your ideas. Without a good approach to problem identification, however, the creative opportunities of the workplace will go unused.

Identifying problems for improvement

- Become aware of problems:
  "Hmm, this is strange."
  "A defect has occurred."
  "This process is inconvenient and time-consuming."

- Have you overlooked these?
  You think of a particular problem every morning before starting the day's work.
  When you start up the job, it never goes smoothly.
  You can't get hold of what you need when you need it.
  There's a drastic difference between busy and slow days.
  Things are not returned to their proper place.
  You feel frustrated because procedures are not followed.
  A measure that works in other work areas doesn't work in yours.
  Prior improvement ideas are not being implemented.
  There's too much waiting and too much waste.
  The same procedure produces varied results.

Look at the workplace with a problem-finding attitude. The workplace will provide ample opportunities for creative problem-solving.

Five main tasks to think about in the workplace:

- How to improve and maintain quality and reduce defects
- How to reduce cost
- How to improve productivity and meet delivery deadlines
- How to increase safety
- How to improve interpersonal relationships

Are there problems with the "four Ms" of the workplace?

- Me
- Machine
- Material
- Method

Are there waste, inadequacy, and inconsistency in the workplace?

- Is the method inadequate?
- Is waste occurring?
- Is there inconsistency in results?

Improvement hints for the week

- Monday: Look for costs that can be reduced
- Tuesday: Look for items requiring improvement
- Wednesday: Look throughout the workplace
- Thursday: Look for hazardous conditions
- Friday: Look for organization and orderliness

Step 2: Research

M misses a step while walking down a staircase and sprains his ankle. You might say that there's nothing more to the injury than carelessness, and you may be right. Many people walk down the same steps, and only M was injured. M says he had just had an argument with Q and was not paying attention to the steps.

However, on investigation, you learn that the steps had just been washed and were still wet. It also turns out that M was not wearing the required rubber-soled shoes and that the staircase, despite its steep angle, was not equipped with a handrail — two factors that could have contributed to M's accident.

Almost anyone would agree that it would be a very superficial analysis to attribute M's injury to his argument with Q. Nevertheless, we tend to assume that the first contributory factor we identify is the sole cause of the problem.

Asking "Why?" Five Times

Careful analysis of an occurrence will usually show there is more than one cause. You will also find a cause of a cause, and a cause of a cause of a cause. The causal chain ultimately extends to infinity.

It is therefore imperative to consider whether the first "cause" you detect for a particular phenomenon is really the true cause. This requires considering all the relevant facts, including the flow of work, the work procedure, the worker's movements, the jigs and fixtures, and the machines and equipment used. For each factor, you must ask the question "Why?" and search for the true cause. What you intuitively feel is the cause is usually not the whole story; the true cause is usually hidden. If you go back at least five "generations" of cause, you will be likely to find the true cause.

QC Tools for Understanding the Current Situation

To solve a problem we must understand it. This means gathering all the relevant facts. The data you collect must be organized to be easily understood. This is especially true when tackling major, deep-rooted problems such as those brought up in group discussion. In such cases, quality control charts and graphs, described in detail in the subsequent pages, should be

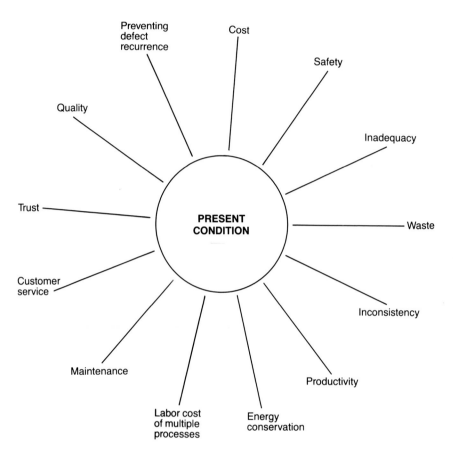

used to make the problem more understandable and to make sure that all group members understand the problem in the same way. Using these QC tools will also lead to a thorough analysis of the workplace, enabling countless new problems to be identified in the course of solving the original problem.

Pareto chart

Pareto analysis sorts raw data into several categories and presents the data on a bar chart arranged in decreasing order. A line graph indicates the cumulative value of the data, ending at 100 percent. Pareto charts are widely used for identifying a problem and understanding the distribution of defects thought to contribute to the problem. They provide information on the number of defects present overall and the percentage each specific defect contributes to the problem as a whole.

QC Tools

1. *Pareto chart* shows the distribution of factors contributing to a problem or situation.
2. *Cause-and-effect diagram* provides a systematic and ordered understanding of the causes of a problem.
3. *Bar graph* makes numbers more meaningful.
4. *Check sheet* helps make a graph based on available data.
5. *Scatter diagram* helps check the correlation among paired data.
6. *Histogram* helps check the frequency distribution.

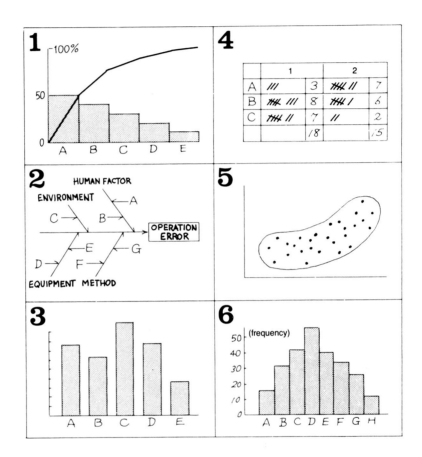

To create a Pareto chart (see page 24):

1. Collect data over a specific period for a specific number of categories.
2. Sort data into categories.
3. Draw the graph.
    a) Draw a horizontal axis (X) and two vertical axes (Y). Set out the categories along the X-axis in decreasing order of magnitude, starting with the largest category at the left. Mark the left Y-axis for the number of occurrences in each category. Mark the right Y-axis for percentage.
    b) Enter the data as a bar chart.
    c) Connect the cumulative values with a line.
4. Analyze and understand the causes and propose countermeasures.

The example shows how we could use Pareto analysis to chart the distribution of Most Valuable Players among American League teams over the last 54 years. This shows us which teams have benefited from the largest number of MVPs.

Pareto Chart: American League MVP Awards by Team (based on data since 1931)

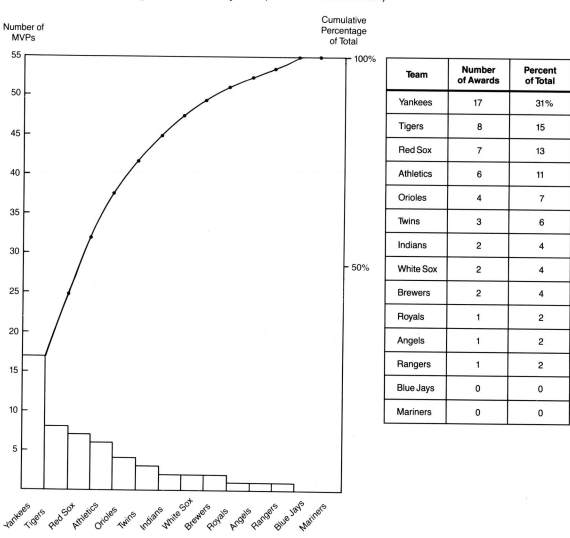

Team	Number of Awards	Percent of Total
Yankees	17	31%
Tigers	8	15
Red Sox	7	13
Athletics	6	11
Orioles	4	7
Twins	3	6
Indians	2	4
White Sox	2	4
Brewers	2	4
Royals	1	2
Angels	1	2
Rangers	1	2
Blue Jays	0	0
Mariners	0	0

Source: *The Complete Handbook of Baseball* (15th ed., Zander Hollander, ed., 1985) Signet Books

Cause-and-effect diagram

The cause-and-effect diagram is used to systematically analyze and organize the causes of a problem. Its purpose is to list the factors that contribute to a result and to organize them from broad to specific factors. It can be used to investigate the causes of defects and suggest solutions or to analyze and correct problems with efficiency or raw cost.

Cause-and-effect diagrams are sometimes referred to as fishbone diagrams because of their shape. The problem or effect to be analyzed is written at the right, where the fish's head would be. The factors that contribute to the effect are written as branches of the main trunk. Major causes are represented as branches directly attached to the main trunk. Smaller branches fanning out from them represent specific influences within each major cause.

To create a cause-and-effect diagram:

1. Identify the result or effect to be addressed and write it on the right of the diagram.
2. Determine the factors that contribute to this effect.
3. Sort the factors into major, minor, and intermediate causes. There is no fast rule about how to sort the factors. As you examine them you will organize them according to the relationships you discover between them.
4. Compare the finished diagram against the actual condition.

As an example, the figure on page 26 shows how to use a cause-and-effect diagram to pinpoint the major and minor causes of a common and frustrating problem — not receiving telephone messages.

Bar graph

Bar graphs are used to analyze the cost of process defects, the number of defects per line, and so forth. Other types of graphs include line graphs, used to show changes in data over time, and pie charts, used to show, for example, the percentage of occurrences of an effect attributable to a specific cause.

Numerical data are more understandable when organized into a bar graph. A good graph must:

Cause-and-Effect Diagram: Missed Telephone Messages

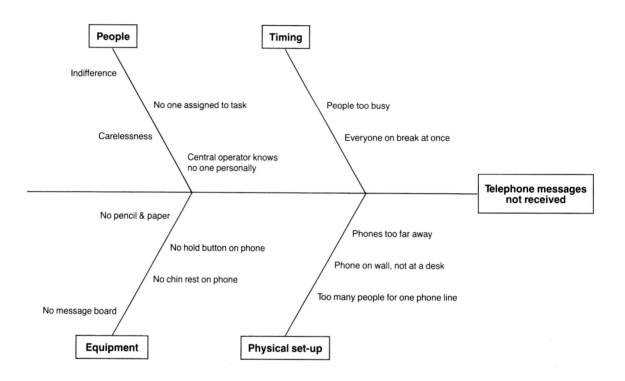

- Provide the overall picture at a single glance;
- Be simple and clear — the meaning of the graph should be obvious;
- Communicate at once — the meaning of the graph should be understandable without explanation;
- Allow the correct interpretation — the scales used, the line thickness, and other such elements must facilitate an accurate judgment about the facts described; and
- Provide a clue for a countermeasure — the graph should suggest the solution to correct the undesirable condition.

Here is a simple example using a bar graph to compare the output of five identical machines on the shop floor. Identifying the least productive machine is the first step toward isolating and correcting the factors causing its poor performance.

Bar Graph: Monthly Stamping Production by Machine

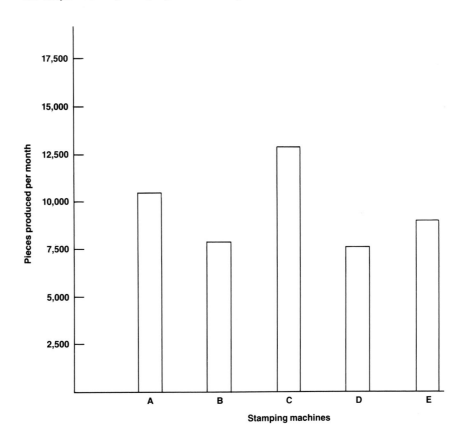

Check sheet

A check sheet is a good way to begin to analyze the causes of a problem. A check sheet is a table for tallying how frequently different events or phenomena occur. It can be used to analyze data about the occurrence of defects or various problems with machines and tools.

A graph is more understandable than a list of numbers. Since it takes time to create a graph, however, it is more efficient to record the data in check sheet form as it is produced. Later the data can be used to make a graph.

Some hints for creating a good check sheet:

- The data should be accurate and easily noted.

- The data must be easily translated into a graph or chart after it is produced.
- The data recorded should be easily presentable as a report.
- The check sheet should convey information not readily express-ible with numbers or words.
- The data must be understandable at a glance.

The example shows how to use a check sheet to chart some of the causes of employee absenteeism.

Check Sheet: Absenteeism

Reason	Division A	Division B	Division C	Annual Total
Illness	卌 卌 卌 卌 卌 卌 卌 卌 卌 ///	卌 卌 卌 卌 卌 //	卌 卌 卌 卌 卌 卌 卌 卌 卌 卌 卌 卌	135
Child Illness	卌 卌 卌 卌 卌 卌	卌 卌 卌 //	卌 卌 卌 卌 卌 //	74
Personal day	卌 卌	卌 ////	卌 卌 卌 //	36
Family death	////	//	////	10
Professional leave	卌 //	卌 卌	////	21
Total	99	65	112	276

Scatter diagram

When you analyze problems in the workplace, you will identify many potential causes, and as you create a cause-and-effect diagram you will discover that some of the causes are related to each other. A scatter diagram is a way of charting paired data to highlight the causal relationships between them.

To create a scatter diagram:

1. Collect pairs of data for two causes or characteristics (A and B) you wish to study. It is good to have as large a sample as possible — at least 20 data pairs.
2. Plot the value for characteristic A along the horizontal axis and that for B along the vertical axis. Make sure the values on these axes include the maximum and minimum values of A and B in your sample.
3. Plot the particular combinations of A and B as points on the graph.
4. Analyze the correlation.
   a) Is there a correlation?
   b) Is it a positive correlation (an increase in A means an increase in B) or an inverse correlation (an increase in A causes a decrease in B)?
   c) Is there a point that does not fit in the pattern of the correlation? Look for some abnormality that may have caused the deviant point.
   d) What is the approximate shape of a line connecting the points?

The figure gives an example of a scatter diagram to check the relationship between employee salaries and years of experience. Monthly salary is plotted along the X-axis and years along the Y-axis. Each point on the diagram represents a particular individual's combination of these two factors.

The distribution of the points in the figure indicates that for this sample group, salary does tend to increase with job experience. Similarly, you could use such a chart to investigate the correlation between the dimensions of sample parts and of finished products made with the part.

Scatter Diagram: Salary and Years of Experience

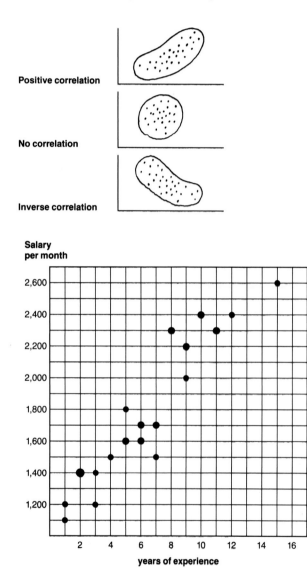

Employee	Years Experience	Salary Per Month
1	2	1400
2	4	1500
3	3	1400
4	9	2000
5	12	2400
6	1	1200
7	7	1700
8	5	1800
9	10	2400
10	11	2300
11	8	2300
12	7	1500
13	15	2600
14	9	2200
15	5	1600
16	3	1200
17	6	1700
18	2	1400
19	1	1150
20	6	1600

Histogram

A histogram is a special type of bar graph showing the frequency distribution of a large number of data. Histograms are frequently used for checking the distribution of a particular dimension of a component part.

A histogram is a convenient way to display at a glance the distribution of various characteristics of a group of data. To create a histogram:

1. Collect data.
2. Sort the collected data into equal-sized classes; for 30 to 50 pieces of data, five to seven classes are usually adequate.
3. Make a tally of the frequency of data in each class.
4. Use the frequency table to draw a bar graph, with the classes along the horizontal axis and the frequency scale along the vertical axis.
5. Check the distribution from the histogram.

The figure is an example of a histogram plotting the distribution of delivery delays of various lengths past the promised date, using number of days behind schedule as the measured class.

Histogram: Distribution of Delivery Delays

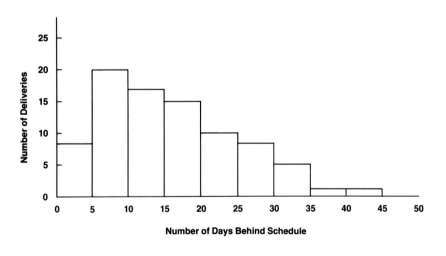

Step 3: Idea Formulation

Unlike mathematical problems, which usually have only one answer, problems dealing with workplace improvement have many possible solutions. The goal is to select the best answer from these possibilities. For this reason, solving an improvement problem is simultaneously easier and harder than solving a math problem.

People frequently ask whether to emphasize quantity or quality in making suggestions. When overall improvement is the goal, it is important initially to formulate as many ideas as possible. The sheer quantity of ideas inevitably leads to quality.

It is important to seek solutions and ideas for a given problem from as many angles as possible. If the problem is to be solved by a group, a brainstorming session should be held to generate as many ideas as possible. If you are working on the problem alone, you should hold a "solo" brainstorming session.

People prefer to maintain the status quo. They like to stay put, retain their viewpoint, and criticize. Such an attitude, however, does not contribute to good ideas, regardless of how well a problem is identified or studied. When you brainstorm, then, don't put a damper on your own or others' ideas by saying, "This is too time-consuming," or "This is too costly." The rule at this stage is to remain open-minded and imaginative, considering any option, no matter how far-fetched. Feasibility should be considered at a later stage.

If a treasure is to be found from a suggestion activity, it must be unearthed during the idea formulation stage, so let your mind run free and come up with lots of ideas.

Basics of Idea Formulation and Applications

Checklist for idea formulation:

- Elimination: What will happen if something is eliminated?
- Reversal: What will happen if something is reversed?
- Normal and abnormal: Is something an abnormality or does it occur all the time?
- Constant and variable: What will happen if only the changing item is treated as an exception?
- Enlargement and reduction: What will happen if something is enlarged or reduced?
- Linking and separating: What will happen if some things are joined or taken apart?

Osborn's Checklist

Described in A. F. Osborn's book, *Applied Imagination* (New York: Scribner's, 1963), this list suggests additional ways to examine and question a machine, part, or process for improvement ideas:

1. **Use it another way.**
   - Is there another way to use it while keeping the current setup?
   - Can anything else be produced?
2. **Borrow an idea from something similar.**
   - Ideas are formed by combining. See if ideas used elsewhere can be adapted to your improvement project.
3. **Change or replace it.**
   - Change the shape, color, sound, smell, movement, location, orientation, power source, and so on.
   - Rotate it.
   - Remove something that's there; add what's not there.
4. **Expand it.**
   - Add something; spend more time; increase the repetition; make it stronger, longer, or thicker; add some other value; double it; duplicate it; increase it; exaggerate it.
5. **Reduce it.**
   - Remove something; make it smaller or stronger; divide it; simplify it; reduce it; lighten it; express it in a more subdued way.
6. **Use alternatives.**
   - Use someone or something else. Use other elements, ingredients, materials, methods, locations, approaches, or tone of voice.
7. **Replace it.**
   - Use different elements or ingredients, dies, layout, sequence, or arrangement. Reverse the cause and effect. Change the pace, speed, or schedule.
8. **Reverse it.**
   - Turn it upside down; invert it; reverse the positions, front and back, positive and negative. Change the roles, orientation, or setup.
9. **Combine it.**
   - Mix it; make an alloy; assemble it.

How to Formulate Ideas

5W2H method

Type	5W2H	Description	Countermeasure
Subject Matter	What?	What is being done? Can this task be eliminated?	Eliminate unnecessary tasks
Purpose	Why?	Why is this task necessary? Clarify the purpose.	
Location	Where?	Where is it being done? Does it have to be done there?	Change the sequence or combination
Sequence	When?	When is the best time to do it? Does it have to be done then?	
People	Who?	Who is doing it? Should someone else do it? Why am I doing it?	
Method	How?	How is it being done? Is this the best method? Is there some other way?	Simplify the task
Cost	How much?	How much does it cost now? What will the cost be after improvement?	Select an improvement method

A number of simple guidelines have been developed to help people or groups generate new ideas. In general, these guidelines urge you to question everything, from every conceivable angle. The figure outlines the 5W2H Method, which stands for the five "w's" — what, why, where, when, and who — and the two "h's" — how and how much.

- Concentration and dispersion: What will happen if some things are concentrated or dispersed?
- Addition and removal: What will happen if something is added or removed?
- Replacement and substitution: Can time spent waiting be used for another purpose?
- Changing the sequence: What will happen if a different assembly procedure is used?
- Parallel and serial: Can two or more things be done at the same time? Can they be done sequentially?
- Differences and similarities: Is there a method to easily separate different things? Is there a method to group similar things?

Elimination: what will happen if something is eliminated?

The ultimate improvement of a task is to discontinue doing it entirely. If the initial objectives can be achieved even after eliminating a task, then performing the task is wasteful. The formulation of statistics is an example of this. Clerical personnel spend hours preparing statistics from data sent from production floors. Most of the time, however, statistics are created without knowing who will be using them or for what purpose, and they sometimes remain unused. This sort of wasteful practice will not occur if the purpose of each task is well understood. It may not be possible to eliminate a task entirely, but you may find a simpler method to achieve the same purpose.

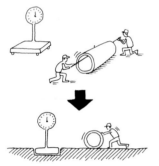

Reversal: what will happen if something is reversed?

A job required two workers to lift an object onto a scale and weigh it. The item was too heavy for one person to lift. Someone then suggested sinking the scale to floor level to eliminate the lifting, so a hole was dug to the right depth and the scale was placed in it. Now, just one worker can roll the item onto the scale.

*Normal and abnormal: is something an abnormality or
does it occur all the time?*

An exception or deviation is an event that occurs rarely. If you want to know how frequently a normal event occurs, it may be quicker to count the number of exceptional events. For example, count the number of people who are absent to know how many people are working. Checking the exception may allow a goal to be reached quicker.

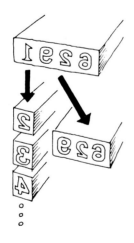

*Constant and variable: what will happen if only the
changing item is treated as an exception?*

Suppose the job is to stamp a serial number starting from 6291. This means that for nine stampings only the last digit changes. Instead of changing the stamp each time, you could do this task by first stamping nine items with "629," the unchanging portion, and then stamping the last digit onto the items. Tasks involving a changing portion and a constant portion can frequently be simplified after considering the two separately.

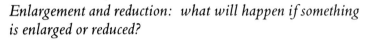

Enlargement and reduction: what will happen if something is enlarged or reduced?

A job may be difficult because it is either very small or very large. If a job is very small, consider using a magnifying lens or a pair of forceps. If something is too large to handle easily, find a way to make it manageable, such as folding it. Consider ways that power tools and other devices can be used to handle the job more easily.

Linking and separating: what will happen if some things are joined or taken apart?

When people screw small parts together, the usual procedure is to grab the screw, start it in the hole by hand, and then tighten it with a screwdriver. You could greatly simplify the job by attaching a tool to the screwdriver that would grab the screw and link it to the screwdriver while you start it in the hole.

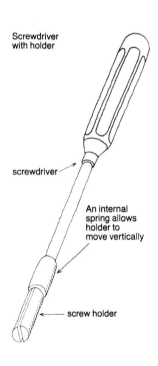

Screwdriver with holder

screwdriver

An internal spring allows holder to move vertically

screw holder

Concentration and dispersion: what will happen if some things are concentrated or dispersed?

Multiple drills and multiple spot-welders make jobs convenient by performing many different tasks at once. On the other hand, dividing a job into different functions may also simplify a job. As an example, imagine the task of gathering a deck of cards that are spread out, some face down and some face up. Rather than picking up all the cards first and then one-by-one flipping over the ones going the wrong way, it would be easier to first pick up the cards facing in the same direction, then gather the remaining cards and stack them together in the same direction.

Addition and removal: what will happen if something is added or removed?

When you tighten a wood screw, the screwdriver may jump out of the slot if the screw is too tight or too shallow. Someone thought of adding a cross-slot for a better grip, and thus the Phillips head screw was invented.

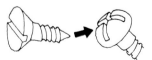

PRESS WORK POSITION

PRESS

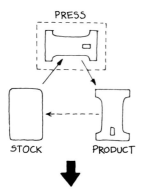

STOCK   PRODUCT

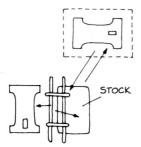

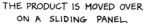

STOCK

THE PRODUCT IS MOVED OVER
ON A SLIDING PANEL.

Replacement and substitution: can time spent waiting be used for another purpose?

Among job motions, unavoidable delay (waiting), empty movement (movement with nothing in hand), and holding (holding an object without moving) are usually easily improved. The figure shows how productivity was significantly improved, eliminating an empty movement by changing the position where pressed products were stored.

Changing the sequence: what will happen if a different assembly procedure is used?

You could put on a necktie in the following steps:

1. Button the shirt,
2. Raise the collar,
3. Position the necktie,
4. Knot the necktie, and
5. Lower the collar.

A better procedure that holds the tie in the right position would be:

1. Raise the collar,
2. Position the necktie,
3. Lower the collar,
4. Knot the necktie, and
5. Button the shirt.

Changing the sequence makes the job easier and keeps the collar from getting as wrinkled.

Parallel and serial: can two or more things be done at the same time? can they be done sequentially?

Instead of washing seven boxes one at a time, you could use a system like the one shown in the figure. The seven boxes are placed in a rack in offset positions so that when soapy water is poured into the top box, it will overflow into the remaining six boxes in succession. This is a good example of eliminating unnecessary processes by a three-dimensional use of space.

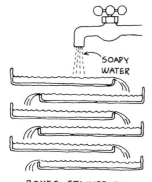

SOAPY
WATER

BOXES STACKED IN
OFFSET POSITION

THREAD-CUTTING MACHINE

OPEN-MESH CHUTE

NUT

NUT

CUTTING WASTE

Differences and similarities: is there a method to easily separate different things? is there a method to group similar things?

The figure depicts a way to use differences in size to automatically sort metal chips from finished nuts. At machine shops, replacement gears used with lathes are sorted by their diameter. To do this, a rod is inserted into the hole in the middle. This is an example of using a shared attribute to group similar things.

Examples of Idea Formulation

The well

A thirsty man came to a well that had a hand pump to get a drink of water. He would pump vigorously, then try to catch the water from the spigot in his palms. Only a few droplets were coming out of the spigot, however, by the time he got his hands in position. The man did this several times before he left, discouraged.

Another man came to the well. Instead of repeating what the first man had done (that is, pump vigorously two or three times and then try to catch water from the spigot), he held the pump with one hand, sealed the spigot opening with the other, and drove the pump two or three times. Then he would release his hand and drink the water held back by his palm.

There are many ways to do something, and some ways work better than others!

Barnacles

☞ *When a battleship returns from a cruise, the hull of the ship is covered with barnacles, making the ship much slower in the water. A similar thing happens with people. Experience is important, but some experience can become "barnacles" — things we're attached to that get in our way. We must learn to separate these "barnacles" from the wisdom gained through experience. The older we get, the harder this becomes. People develop fixed ideas of how the navy, its fleet, or its tactics should always be.*

What is scary is not that the individual has fixed ideas, but that the person sitting comfortably in the commander's or the admiral's chair does not know that he has fixed ideas. (Ryotaro Shiba, Saka no Ue no Kumo)

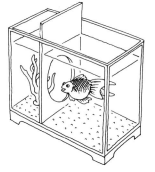

Goldfish

A partition with a hole just big enough for a goldfish to swim through is placed in a goldfish tank. When you place food on the side of the partition away from the goldfish, eventually it will learn to swim through the hole to the food. When you remove the partition after some time, the goldfish will still swim where the hole had been. People are like that goldfish — there are many things that people continue to do out of habit despite changes in the environment.

Ideas must be communicated

About 600 B.C., before the invention of the printing press, a Greek philosopher named Miletus discovered that rubbing amber would create static electricity, which could be used to lift wheat straw. It took 2500 more years to develop the radios and telephones we enjoy today. If a printing press had been available back in Miletus' time to spread the news of his discovery, modern civilization might have come about more quickly. The same thing applies to your good ideas. To have them recognized as good ideas, you must write them down and submit them as suggestions. An idea that is not expressed is almost valueless.

Hexagonal pencils

Look at the pencil on your desk. It probably has a hexagonal cross-section. When pencils were first invented, they had a circular cross-section. Round pencils are still used in special applications, but most are hexagonal. Have you ever wondered why?

Round pencils are easy to hold in the hand, but they tend to roll when you set them down. If pencils had a triangular or square cross-section they wouldn't roll as much, but they would be harder to write with. The hexagonal shape is a compromise between a round shape that is easy to write with and an angular shape that keeps the pencil from rolling.

There are numerous examples such as this around us.

Step 4: Idea Modification

There are many possible answers to problems that require improvement. The criteria to use for honing in on the best solution come from the benefits produced by various answers. More specifically, you must consider factors such as the feasibility of implementation and the cost, time, and labor required, balancing these factors against the benefits of implementation, the adaptability to other situations, and the expected life of the benefits.

If the net benefit is too small or absent, the idea will not be accepted. You may need to refine the idea by finding ways to reduce the cost, make better use of waste, or make the benefits last longer. You shouldn't expect every idea to be implemented. Many are "rough drafts" that must be discarded or polished further. However, ideas that are discarded serve as seeds for future ideas. You may simply need to broaden your perspective and deepen your knowledge and experience. The quality and the depth of your improvement activity depend on your sowing many seeds.

In Japanese painting known as *Iwaegu*, the individual layers of pigment are so light that the paper below is visible for the first few layers. However, by laying many coats one on another, artists create works with a depth, lustre, and presence unmatched by more opaque oil paintings.

In a similar way, a person's wisdom and understanding represent an accumulation of layers of experience and insight deepened by variety and perspective. Good ideas are produced through numerous experiences of trial and error, while a passing idea is usually nothing more than that. Unless you have the courage to reevaluate and even discard the ideas you have, you will not enjoy the fruits of a really successful idea.

Factors Used in Evaluating Ideas

Knowing the factors used in evaluating your ideas is knowing what your company is looking for in suggestions. If you don't know what the company is looking for, you could make suggestions that completely miss the mark. You should evaluate your own ideas with these factors in mind before you submit

Idea Evaluation Factors

Benefits to actual task (contribution to management)	1. Tangible benefits Benefits that can be measured financially, such as increased revenue or productivity, or reduced manpower, time, material, or processing requirements 2. Intangible benefits Benefits that cannot be measured financially, such as reduced workload or improvement in quality, delivery time, safety, cleanliness, orderliness, morale, interpersonal relations, corporate image, or customer trust
Feasibility (difficulty of implementation)	The time and resources needed to implement the idea; the urgency of implementation (should it be implemented immediately or gradually?)
Adaptability	Whether the idea can be used in other workplaces in the company
Other effects	Whether implementing the suggestion will detrimentally affect other workplaces or processes
Continuity	Whether the benefits of the suggestion are long-lasting or transitory
Completeness	Whether the suggestion is concrete enough to implement immediately without modifications or additional work
Originality	Whether the idea is original and creative, an adaptation of an existing idea, or merely an imitation of a prior idea
Research effort	The amount of research, trial and error, and other efforts expended by the suggester. Is the suggestion just a passing thought or does it represent adversities overcome through courage and effort?
Suggestions pertaining to others' workplaces (negative value)	What is the relationship between the suggestion and the suggester's position? What effort was spent in the suggestion, judged from the position of the suggester?

them as suggestions. This will show what your idea lacks and what you should consider further.

The evaluation factors and the weights assigned to each of them vary from company to company, but most companies use some combination of the factors shown in the accompanying table.

Step 5: Implementing the Improvement Plan

More and more companies are using the "implemented suggestion" system — ideas must be put into effect before credit or a reward will be given. This sometimes reflects an improvement in the suggestion-making skill of the employees, but it also may happen when the number of unimplemented "idea" suggestions becomes too large to be centrally managed by a single department.

These two factors are a driving force to get employees to actually implement their improvement ideas. Doing everything — from making suggestions, to implementing them, to confirming the benefits — completes the suggestion cycle, which is more satisfying for the suggesters.

If at all possible, employees should implement their own suggestions after getting proper approvals from management. The exact benefits of an improvement are never known until it is implemented, and employees can learn a lot while checking the actual results of their suggestions.

In an implementation system, the worker obtains the approval and advice of supervisors, and then implements his or her suggestion with the cooperation of colleagues and the technical staff. The new activity provides a chance for the suggester to develop new interpersonal relationships, skills, and experiences that would not have been possible while performing routine jobs. Placing a worker in a new setting gives that person a chance to grow as a human being.

Workers should appreciate that management undertakes significant risks in permitting implementation of improvement plans before examining them as suggestions. The fact that management permits ideas to be implemented on the simple approval and advice of supervisors shows a great trust in the employees' abilities and in their value for the company.

As a suggester, you must give careful consideration to the effects your improvement plan may have on other workers and on the earlier and later processes. It takes patience to achieve the intended benefits of an improvement plan.

Cautions regarding implementation of improvement plans

- *Obtain your supervisor's approval.*
- *Obtain or prepare the things you need for implementation.*
- *With group improvement plans, make individual responsibilities clear.*
- *Establish a daily schedule for the improvement plan.*

- *Notify everyone who might be affected by the improvement plan before you begin implementation.* Improvements entail changes in the status quo. People who are used to an old way may resist the new ways. Therefore, it is important to obtain the prior consent of those who will be affected by the improvement plan or to ask them to take part in the implementation.
- *Establish a trial period.* The implementation of an improvement plan must not adversely affect other departments or processes. The improvement plan should first be tried in a pilot project that is limited to your area and does not affect others.
- *Understand and deal with problems that occur during implementation.* No improvement is 100 percent effective on the first try. In most cases, new and unexpected problems will surface during implementation. Overcoming unexpected problems and completing implementation within the scheduled period are a part of implementing the improvement plan.
- *Seek the advice of your supervisors and the technical staff.* In most cases, professional knowledge and specific experience are required for solving the problems you encounter while implementing an improvement plan. Do not cling to the idea of "doing it on your own." If a problem seems overwhelming, always seek the advice or help of your supervisor and the technical or engineering staff.

Implement yourself what you can do yourself.

Step 6: Follow-Up on the Improvement Plan

After an improvement plan is implemented, you must follow up on the results. We implement improvements with specific goals in mind, such as making jobs easier, improving efficiency, or reducing costs. It is important to check if your improvement plan is achieving the desired objectives, since it is possible for an improvement plan to have detrimental effects.

Following up on an improvement plan is, naturally, the obligation of the person who implemented it. The plan is not completely implemented until the effects of the improvement are checked. Moreover, understanding these effects is indispensable to understanding the overall value of the improvement plan.

Improvement Follow-Up

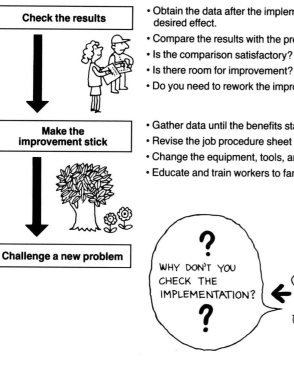

Check the results

• Obtain the data after the implementation. Check whether the idea produced the desired effect.
• Compare the results with the pre-improvement figures.
• Is the comparison satisfactory?
• Is there room for improvement?
• Do you need to rework the improvement plan?

Make the improvement stick

• Gather data until the benefits stabilize. Make corrections if necessary.
• Revise the job procedure sheet to reflect the new method.
• Change the equipment, tools, and other surrounding conditions to fit the new procedure.
• Educate and train workers to familiarize them with the new procedure.

Challenge a new problem

If the results are not satisfactory, it may be necessary to go back to the beginning and start the improvement process over. This usually isn't necessary with small improvement plans that were well formulated in the beginning. However, achieving the desired results becomes more difficult as the complexity of the improvement plan increases.

After you are able to confirm that the desired effects are being achieved, you must communicate the improvement to avoid a regression to the old way of doing things. Unless changes in tasks or improvements in machines and tools are publicized, written in work standard sheets, and made familiar to all workers, the improved procedures or equipment can easily be forgotten, neglected, and gradually replaced by the past practices.

An improvement is not complete until every step, including follow-up, is implemented. Some of the steps outlined above may be superfluous when implementing simple improvements such as placing something on the left side of the worker that had previously been on the right. Even in such a case, however, the steps must be followed in a more abbreviated form. Those who only make idea suggestions and do not implement them should nevertheless become familiar with the steps described so that they can make a complete improvement when the time comes for them to do so.

Famous Quotations about Ideas

☞ *I have never done anything of worth by coincidence. None of my inventions have come as a result of coincidence. They were hard work. (Thomas Edison)*

☞ *Man can put out about 1/20 of a horsepower. He has to rest at least 9 hours a day. He also has to eat and drink. As a power source, we are terrible. However, it is when man starts thinking of ideas that the difference between man and machine emerges. (Soichiro Honda)*

☞ *Ideas are born amidst the noise of machines and work. (Kiyoshi Ichimura)*

☞ *The innovative organization requires a learning atmosphere throughout the entire business. It creates and maintains continuous learning. No one is allowed to consider himself "finished" at any time. Learning is a continuing process for all members of the organization. (Peter Drucker,* Management: Tasks, Responsibilities, Practices*)*

☞ *People show tremendous abilities when they are pushed to the very limit. A person who is always the point man usually comes up with good ideas. (Yajiro Ikari)*

☞ *There is no joy other than the joy of creating. There is no man who is truly alive other than one who is creating. All others are just shadows on the earth with nothing to do with being alive. The joy of living, whether it is love or action, is the joy of creating. (Romain Rolland)*

☞ *Failure allows a researcher to obtain valuable experience and expand his ideas to infinity. (Masafumi Inoki)*

CHAPTER 3

How to
Write Suggestions

When you left school, you may have thought that you were no longer going to use your writing skills. But a suggestion system asks that you continue to use these skills. Some suggestion systems allow oral reports, but most require you to write down the suggestion using a prescribed form.

Suggestions are examined and evaluated on the merits of what you write in the form. Once the suggestion form leaves your hands, whether your suggestion is accepted and whether you receive recognition or a reward depend solely on the information you provide in the form.

Your suggestion is not the only one the examiner receives. Any examiner is flooded with volumes of suggestions and will have to read and evaluate it in only a fraction of the time you spent writing it. Unless the problems, your improvement idea, and the benefits of the improvement are clearly set forth, even the most generous and intelligent examiner will find it impossible to understand your vision. Making a clear presentation to the examiner is not only a basic courtesy — it is also indispensable for conveying the full value of your suggestion. Remember that the way the suggestion is written may double the value of your suggestion or reduce it to zero.

It is said that each color used on a suggestion form is worth an additional $5 in reward money. This is an exaggeration, of course, but it is true that communication techniques, whether additional colors or some other detail, are important for drawing the examiner's attention to the value and creativity of your idea.

Key elements of a good suggestion

- Be sure to fill in all items on the form.
- Think of the person who will be reading it. Write legibly and dark. Check for missing or misspelled words.
- Draw attention to important points by underlining or using a different color. For example:
  a) Write important points in red.
  b) Indicate electrodes in yellow.
  c) Indicate cylinder-related parts in blue.
  d) With figures, indicate the work piece in green.
  e) Indicate jigs and fixtures in brown.

- Make the title concrete enough to give a good idea of the contents.
- Describe the current situation (the situation prior to improvement):
  - a) Make sure the problem is clearly defined.
  - b) State What → How → Why the improvement is necessary.
  - c) Be as specific as possible and make your point clear.
  - d) Add illustrations for better understanding.
  - e) Be quantitative in your discussion for greater clarity.

- Describe the improvement plan (details of your improvement idea):
  - a) Be brief but clear in describing the difference between the improvement plan and the current situation.
  - b) For clarity, add illustrations to show the "before" and "after" conditions.
  - c) Quantify your discussion where appropriate.
  - d) Describe the necessary preparation, materials, and cost of the improvement.
  - e) Don't forget to include your own opinion.
  - f) Describe the process by which you arrived at your improvement plan. Describe the difficulties you had, the failures you had, and so on. This will make it easier to evaluate your improvement plan. For example:
    1.) The first modification involved X, but this didn't produce the expected improvements.
    2.) The second modification created a new set of problems.
    3.) The third modification is the improvement plan. It corrects the problems created by the second modification.

- Describe the benefits:
  - a) Describe the benefits from the most beneficial to the least. Cover a wide spectrum, touching on safety, cost, number of process steps, quality, service, and so on. Because benefits are interrelated, as shown in the hexagonal diagram, look at the improvement from different

perspectives to uncover as many benefits as possible.

b) Use numbers and figures for clarity, stating the appropriate units (per day, per month, per piece, etc.).

c) If the improvement involves reducing the number of process steps, suggest ways in which the machines or workers used in eliminated process steps can be used.

d) State whether the improvement plan has been implemented and is actually being used.

e) Remember to propose uses of the improvement plan in different departments if appropriate.

See "How to Improve Suggestion Writing Style" on pages 60-61.

Interrelated Benefits of Improvements

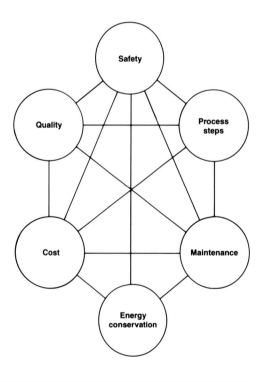

Writing Style

Consider the three suggestions shown in the example on page 52. You will notice that example 2 is better than example 1 and example 3 better than example 2 in making a clear, concise

Example 1	Example 2	Example 3
Current condition I perform __(task)__ using the following procedure: 1. _____ , 2. _____ , and 3. _____ . __(The problem)__ was occurring.	**Current condition** I perform __(task)__ using the following procedure: 1. _____ , 2. _____ , and 3. _____ . __(Defect "A")__ was occurring. 1. __(Defect "A")__ was occurring at the rate of _____ times per day. 2. __(Defect "B")__ was occurring about _____ times per day.	**Current situation** I perform _____ at the __(task)__ , which had the following problems: 1. __(Defect "A")__ was occurring at the rate of _____ per day. 2. _____ was poor and _____ was occurring at the rate of _____ per _____ . 3. _____ was poor and _____ was occurring.
Improvement The work procedure for __(task)__ has been changed as follows: 1. _____ , 2. _____ , 3. _____ .	**Improvement** The work procedure for __(task)__ has been changed as follows: 1. _____ , 2. _____ , 3. _____ . Before improvement: 1. _____ 2. _____ 3. _____ After improvement: 1. _____ 2. _____ 3. _____ "Before" sketch → "After" sketch	**Improvement** The problems were solved by changing _____ and _____ to _____ . Before improvement: 1. _____ 2. _____ 3. _____ After improvement: 1. _____ 2. _____ 3. _____ (More detailed "before" drawing) → (More detailed "after" drawing)
Benefits __(The problem)__ does not occur any more. __(The procedure)__ has been improved.	**Benefits** 1. The occurrence of __(Defect "A")__ has been reduced to _____ times per day. 2. _____ occurs only _____ times a day. 3. _____ has been improved.	**Benefits** 1. __(Defect "A")__ has been reduced from a rate of _____ to _____ . 2. _____ was improved and _____ was reduced by _____ per _____ . (Indicate an equation, calculating rate per day, per month, or per piece, for example). 3. The improved work procedure has led to work standardization and better ability to locate defects occurring in an earlier process. 4. Reliability of __(task)__ has been increased. This improvement can also be used with __(second task)__ .

expression of the suggestion theme and an orderly presentation of the type of information the examiners are looking for.

In example 1, the writer says that an improvement was made. In example 3, however, the writer exhibits a greater understanding of the need for an improvement — she states clearly that the improvement has solved the problems and describes the benefits of the improvement. Example 3 is a more convincing statement than example 1. Remember that the value of an improvement can be multiplied or diminished by the way it is written.

Illustration

In most cases, the suggestion examiner does not know the details of the shop floor. He or she almost certainly knows less than you do about the situation you are trying to improve or have improved. It is therefore best for you to use illustrations to ensure that your improvement is fully understood by the examiner.

Visual communication is a powerful tool. One illustration can convey the equivalent of dozens or even hundreds of words. A drawing presents information immediately in a very unambiguous way.

Vivid Presentation

B wanted to make suggestions but lacked the ability to express his thoughts. He would write suggestions diligently, but they never clearly expressed what he intended to say. His suggestions were not evaluated highly.

B's supervisor suggested he use graphic, step-by-step illustrations such as the ones in the figure on page 55. With practice, anyone can draw this kind of sketch. The addition of clear illustrations makes the suggestion much more vivid and understandable to the examiner.

Concrete Presentation of the Effects

An improvement that you may consider minor may have far-reaching but less noticeable effects when viewed from the proper perspective. Do not hesitate to write as many effects as

Uses of Illustration

The shape of an object is better understood with a three-dimensional figure. To ensure the best understanding, also draw the front view, the plane view, and the side view.

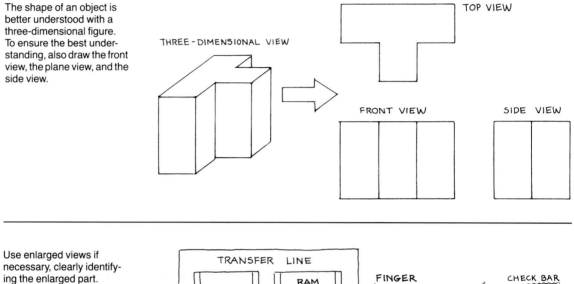

Use enlarged views if necessary, clearly identifying the enlarged part.

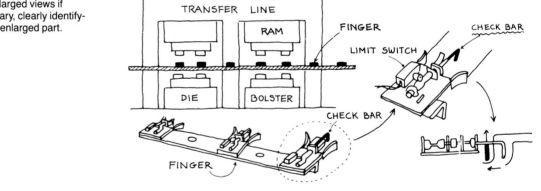

This example shows an improvement in the position used to check a dimension. With the position used before the improvement, a leftward shift in the work piece would move it out of position for measurement. When the work piece is measured from the improved direction, the measurement position coincides with the center of the work piece, easily accommodating a shift to either side.

Use colors or shading to clearly identify a change in shape, position, direction, or the like, if the improvement is not obvious.

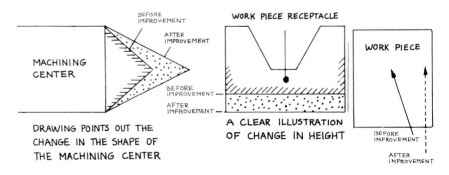

Making Graphic Presentations

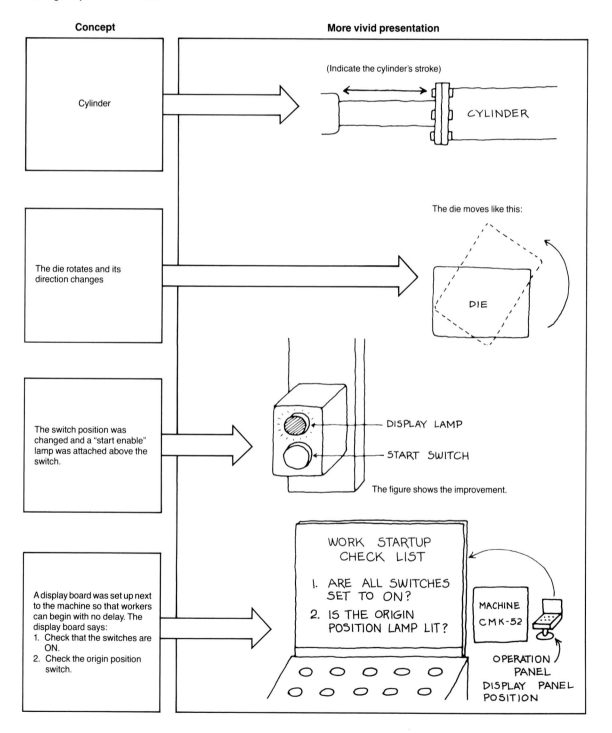

you can think of. This does not mean exaggerating the benefits of the improvement, but you should consider and express the fullest significance of the improvement.

The goals of a shop floor, whether quality, safety, cost, delivery deadline, or some other objective, are not independent but related. Their interrelationship must be well understood in order to comprehend the full effect of an improvement. Trying to understand all of the effects of an improvement is also a way of understanding the interrelationship among different activities and their purposes.

Guidelines for Presenting Effects of the Improvement

---

1. Be as specific as possible.

Improved Safety:	• Reduced injury to legs from inadvertently striking object • No more tripping over object • Fewer injuries due to inattentiveness

---

2. Quantify if possible. Express cost savings in dollars and cents.

• Indicate the equations used

• Check the unit cost of the materials, parts, energy, jigs, and fixtures in advance

• Convert the time saved by improved productivity and so forth into a dollar amount, using the cost of labor as a guide

Decreased line stoppage →	Before improvement: 2/month × 0.5 hour/worker × \$14/hour = \$14/month After improvement: 0/month = \$0/month
Eliminating damage to cutting tools →	Damage to cutting tools, which averaged ten per month at \$25 per tool, was eliminated, saving \$250 per month

---

3. List all effects. For example, the effects of eliminating damage to cutting tools include:

• Reducing the number of defective work pieces previously made by the damaged tools (indicate the monetary savings)

• Eliminating machine stoppage due to tool damage (indicate the monetary savings in labor previously used to correct the problem)

• Improving worker safety — fewer injuries to hands, legs, and so on (quantify by number of hours previously lost due to accidents involving damaged cutting tools)

Unwelcome Suggestions

To understand the types of suggestions likely to be viewed favorably by the management, let's consider the types of suggestions that are not welcomed.

Abstract, imaginary suggestions

Suggestions must be realistic — they must produce tangible benefits when implemented. Imagination and free-thinking are important when you are searching for ideas, but the idea itself must embody a concrete improvement to a real problem before it is submitted as a suggestion. It's okay to think, "This tiresome job should be automated." Before the thought is presented as a suggestion, however, you must consider, for example, what machine should be used and the range of tasks to be mechanized. You must also consider the cost of automation, the expected improvement in efficiency, the use of the surplus time, the problems of automation itself, and so on. There are many aspects to consider and numerous problems to solve before your idea is ready to become a suggestion.

Opinions, wishes, and complaints

An example of this type is: "The soup at the cafeteria is 'too salty' or 'too sweet.'" Such a statement is highly subjective and is not accompanied by any suggestion for improvement. If the writer truly feels that the soup at the cafeteria is too salty or sweet, he should investigate how objective his opinion is and

what real problems are caused by the soup being too salty or sweet. The writer should then think of the corrective measures. He may find that his opinion about the soup is not shared by others and is not caused simply by the amount of salt.

Personnel issues such as work hours, wages, performance evaluation, and transfer

Regrettably, most management groups are not open to suggestion on personnel matters from the workers at large. Human resources decisions affect all workers and must be well coordinated to work for the entire company. If personnel decisions were based simply on suggestions by workers, the organization would lose its order and harmony. Personnel matters should be discussed in individual meetings with one's supervisor or communicated to management through whatever channels have been established for that purpose. The suggestion system does not have a mandate to alter human resources policy.

Suggestions that do not lead to improvements

Suggestions that delegate greater authority to the workers or that have detrimental effects on other departments or processes should never be adopted. However, it is not unusual for an idea that appears to be an improvement from a microscopic viewpoint actually to be harmful from a macroscopic point of view. Suggestions should therefore be evaluated by examiners who are trained to consider the larger picture.

Suggestions that are similar

Adopting ideas used in other companies or other departments is encouraged. The process of studying prior ideas, understanding them, combining them with other ideas, and incorporating them as your own idea spreads the benefits of an improvement and makes full use of the initial idea.

Adapting an idea to your workplace requires creativity. Nevertheless, using the same improvement based on the same thinking process to improve the same type of condition is nothing more than copying. Copying may produce benefits, but it doesn't involve adding new ideas. It is very difficult to draw a clear line between copying an idea and adapting an idea. In general, however, it is better to avoid presenting a previous solution for the same type of job as a suggestion unless you have improved on it with your own ideas.

Divided suggestions

If two or more pieces of a particular type of equipment have the same problems or if the same problems occur in different places, it would be natural to consider the problems as one and the same. It is possible, of course, for a problem to be composed of a set of smaller problems, in which case it may be better to solve the smaller problems one by one. But unless there is a rational reason such as that, a single problem affecting many machines or a single problem occurring at many places should be considered a single problem to be solved by a single suggestion.

Submitting five separate suggestions for five pieces of equipment facing the same problem is nothing more than "suggestion-padding" and should be avoided. Making multiple suggestions out of what should really be a single suggestion increases the load on the examiners and may actually reduce the synergistic effect the whole idea would have presented, thereby lowering the value of the suggestion. Suggestions should actually be as comprehensive as possible. Comprehensiveness is one measure of their quality. Don't be so concerned with the reward or recognition given for suggestions that you focus only on the number you make.

Suggestions requiring a large investment

It is probably incorrect to state categorically that all suggestions entailing large investments are undesirable. The value of a suggestion is equal to the difference between the benefit and the cost involved, and a large investment may be justified by a larger benefit. However, it is common sense in management that substantial investments should produce substantial benefits. If a suggestion can produce the benefit with less investment, the suggestion is that much more valuable. Production floor employees should make a primary goal of searching for suggestions that improve problems without requiring large investments.

How to Improve Suggestion Writing Style

• **Current condition:** Water droplets form on the plumbing leading to the die used with the 232 grill, run into the die, and cause defective products. • **Improvement:** Thermal insulation material was wrapped around the plumbing. • **Effect:** Water droplets from the plumbing do not run into the die. Defects have been eliminated.	**(Improvement)**

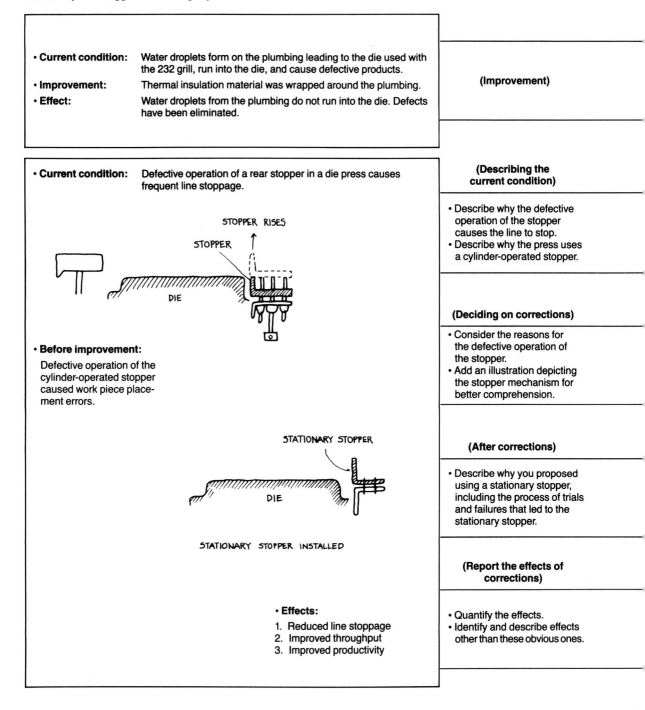

• **Current condition:** Defective operation of a rear stopper in a die press causes frequent line stoppage.	**(Describing the current condition)**
	• Describe why the defective operation of the stopper causes the line to stop. • Describe why the press uses a cylinder-operated stopper.
	(Deciding on corrections)
• **Before improvement:** Defective operation of the cylinder-operated stopper caused work piece placement errors.	• Consider the reasons for the defective operation of the stopper. • Add an illustration depicting the stopper mechanism for better comprehension.
	(After corrections)
	• Describe why you proposed using a stationary stopper, including the process of trials and failures that led to the stationary stopper.
	(Report the effects of corrections)
• **Effects:** 1. Reduced line stoppage 2. Improved throughput 3. Improved productivity	• Quantify the effects. • Identify and describe effects other than these obvious ones.

In the illustrations: STOPPER RISES, STOPPER, DIE, STATIONARY STOPPER, DIE, STATIONARY STOPPER INSTALLED

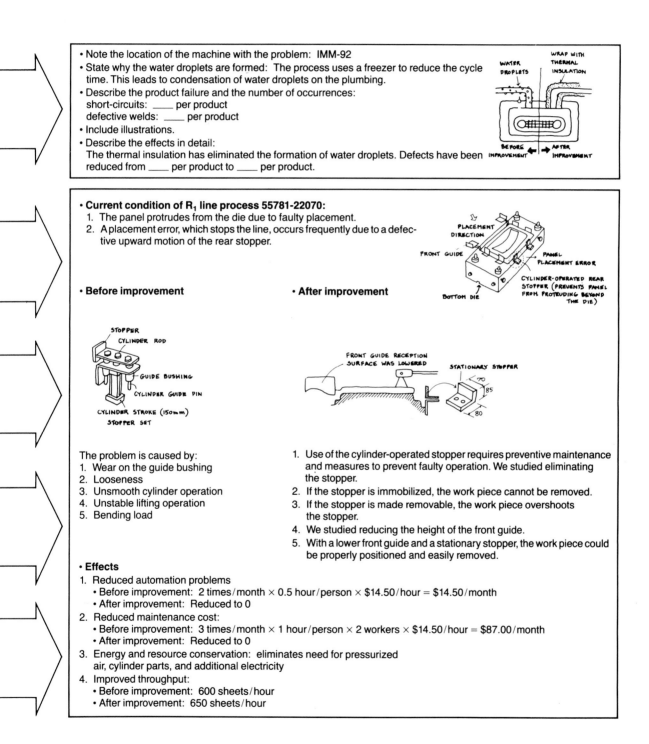

- Note the location of the machine with the problem: IMM-92
- State why the water droplets are formed: The process uses a freezer to reduce the cycle time. This leads to condensation of water droplets on the plumbing.
- Describe the product failure and the number of occurrences:
  short-circuits: ____ per product
  defective welds: ____ per product
- Include illustrations.
- Describe the effects in detail:
  The thermal insulation has eliminated the formation of water droplets. Defects have been reduced from ____ per product to ____ per product.

- **Current condition of R$_1$ line process 55781-22070:**
  1. The panel protrudes from the die due to faulty placement.
  2. A placement error, which stops the line, occurs frequently due to a defective upward motion of the rear stopper.

- **Before improvement**

- **After improvement**

The problem is caused by:
1. Wear on the guide bushing
2. Looseness
3. Unsmooth cylinder operation
4. Unstable lifting operation
5. Bending load

1. Use of the cylinder-operated stopper requires preventive maintenance and measures to prevent faulty operation. We studied eliminating the stopper.
2. If the stopper is immobilized, the work piece cannot be removed.
3. If the stopper is made removable, the work piece overshoots the stopper.
4. We studied reducing the height of the front guide.
5. With a lower front guide and a stationary stopper, the work piece could be properly positioned and easily removed.

- **Effects**
1. Reduced automation problems
   - Before improvement: 2 times/month × 0.5 hour/person × $14.50/hour = $14.50/month
   - After improvement: Reduced to 0
2. Reduced maintenance cost:
   - Before improvement: 3 times/month × 1 hour/person × 2 workers × $14.50/hour = $87.00/month
   - After improvement: Reduced to 0
3. Energy and resource conservation: eliminates need for pressurized air, cylinder parts, and additional electricity
4. Improved throughput:
   - Before improvement: 600 sheets/hour
   - After improvement: 650 sheets/hour

CHAPTER 4

How to Improve Suggestions

Jumping to the Next Step
  Development Stages in K's Suggestion Activity
Recording Your Ideas
Making Problems Visible
Setting Goals
Suggestion Competitions
Self-Improvement
Making Group Suggestions
Suggestion-Improvement Activities:
  Personal Experiences

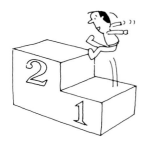

Jumping to the Next Step

When you began to participate in the suggestion system, you probably started out with the idea, "I'm going to make every suggestion I can." You probably looked around and suggested whatever came to your mind. In those days you may have believed that if you made enough suggestions, a few of them were bound to be good.

However, as you continue making suggestions over time, you begin to realize what the suggestion system is all about and what your role is in the company as a whole. You probably understand these things in a personal way, much better than if you read about or were told about them. This is the beauty of the suggestion system.

As you start understanding what makes a good suggestion, you gain a sense of what management is looking for from its worker improvement activity. Is it energy conservation? Cost reduction? A reduced work force? What should the workers stress in their work?

Management's improvement priorities should be clear even before you are familiar with the suggestion system, but your intuitive understanding of management's needs will increase with your understanding of the suggestion system. Naturally, if your suggestions address what management is most interested in, they will be more highly evaluated.

When you can make suggestions that are timely and relevant to management needs, you have reached the second stage. Here, you are no longer looking around desperately for minor changes to suggest. Instead, you are looking for improvements from a much broader perspective. This process gives you a sense of personal growth that you will enjoy and want to continue.

At this point you are ready to begin rapid progress. You should welcome self-education and self-improvement with open arms. There are books to read, techniques to improve, and outside seminars to attend — so much to learn and do!

Development Stages in K's Suggestion Activity

First five years with the company: In the beginning, my suggestions were not accepted for implementation. However, I was glad that my supervisors were paying attention to the ideas I was presenting. I submitted my suggestions after making sure they were well written and that the words were used correctly. After a while, I started receiving rewards for my suggestions and my supervisors encouraged me, motivating me to make more suggestions.

Five to ten years: I learned about the company's commendation system. I made up my mind to win an award, and even though I had changed jobs to join this company, I did win the annual award and a quarterly award. This gave me confidence and motivated me to work harder.

Ten to fifteen years: I thought it would be better to work with my colleagues on improvements. So we formed a suggestion group at our workplace where we can discuss creative ideas in a relaxed atmosphere. As a result of this activity, my colleagues and I have won the company award. The joint suggestion activity has helped our subordinates learn their jobs, and the workplace is becoming alive. This has been very gratifying.

Recording Your Ideas

As you are working on an improvement activity, you sometimes forget some of the specific ideas you have. The idea may be on the tip of your tongue, but you just can't remember it. Everybody has had this frustrating experience.

It is said that people absorb new ideas and experience by forgetting some of their past memories. To successfully participate in an improvement system, however, you should not forget any of your ideas, even if they are something as trivial as an unsafe work practice or a single missing screw.

Forgetfulness can be solved by devising some method for storing your ideas. It may be a notebook that you use to write down whatever problems you observe or changes you think of. Don't kill an idea at the beginning, saying that something won't work. Write it down first. You never know what will come in handy later. But once you write down a fact, delete it from your consciousness so that you can devote your awareness to making new observations.

In writing this chapter, we borrowed an "idea notebook" from one of the best suggesters at Toyota. This rather plain black notebook was worn out, with the cover hanging by a few strands of thread. It was a beautifully well-used notebook. Its pages, smeared with machine oil, were filled with diagrams and memos. Problems the employee identified were written down as he saw them. He gave each problem a careful trial-and-error research to find the right way of correcting it. The notebook is really the embodiment of this person's efforts in the improvement activity.

Example of an Idea Memo

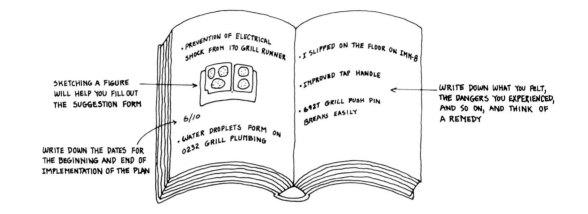

SKETCHING A FIGURE WILL HELP YOU FILL OUT THE SUGGESTION FORM

WRITE DOWN THE DATES FOR THE BEGINNING AND END OF IMPLEMENTATION OF THE PLAN

- PREVENTION OF ELECTRICAL SHOCK FROM 170 GRILL RUNNER

6/10

- WATER DROPLETS FORM ON 0232 GRILL PLUMBING

- I SLIPPED ON THE FLOOR ON IMM-8
- IMPROVED TAP HANDLE
- 692T GRILL PUSH PIN BREAKS EASILY

WRITE DOWN WHAT YOU FELT, THE DANGERS YOU EXPERIENCED, AND SO ON, AND THINK OF A REMEDY

S's Idea Notebook

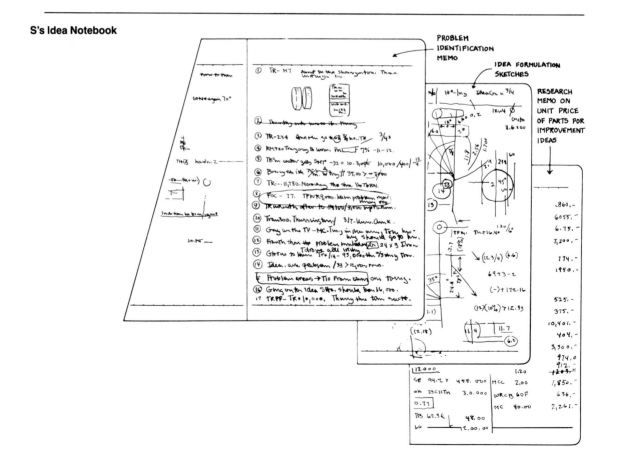

PROBLEM IDENTIFICATION MEMO

IDEA FORMULATION SKETCHES

RESEARCH MEMO ON UNIT PRICE OF PARTS FOR IMPROVEMENT IDEAS

Making Problems Visible

As you improve the small defects that surround you, you start running out of problems. Things become cleaner, more orderly, and better organized. Problems are no longer readily apparent, and you may feel that there is nothing left to improve.

This is only an illusion. Problems persist in the workplace. If you cannot find a problem, you lack either the skill to identify it or sufficient information.

For example, do you know the cost of the raw material including parts, tools, energy, and office supplies that you use at

Look at Unit Costs — They Add Up!

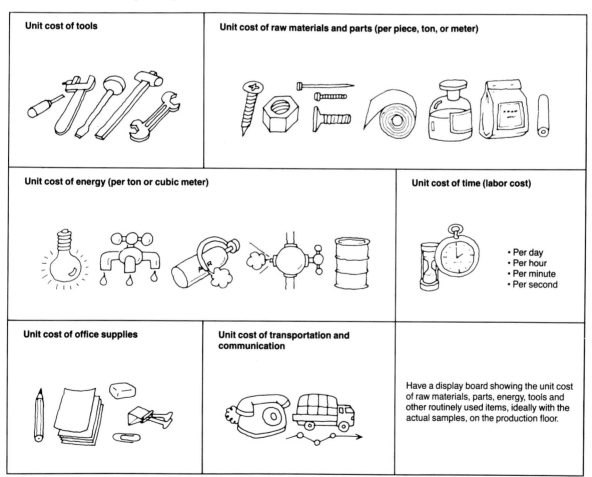

Unit cost of tools

Unit cost of raw materials and parts (per piece, ton, or meter)

Unit cost of energy (per ton or cubic meter)

Unit cost of time (labor cost)
• Per day
• Per hour
• Per minute
• Per second

Unit cost of office supplies

Unit cost of transportation and communication

Have a display board showing the unit cost of raw materials, parts, energy, tools and other routinely used items, ideally with the actual samples, on the production floor.

your workplace? When a problem occurs and you correct it, do you analyze the root cause? If you don't have all the necessary information — if you don't look deep enough — your solutions will not be incisive enough. You may feel there is nothing more to improve once superficial improvements are made.

Tomokazu Hori of Matsushita Electric, who is credited with making 4,000 suggestions in one year, has said that if you think hard enough, you can come up with a limitless number of potential improvements to a single screw. Hori himself studied the relative cost, strength, and appearance of using a slotted head versus a Phillips head, a flat-head screw versus an Allen screw, screws of different lengths, and screws with washers.

In today's production environment, problems that are immediately obvious to everyone are almost non-existent. As problems are solved, it becomes more difficult to make improvements without careful thought. You must collect information well and look for problems systematically.

Setting Goals

A, who has participated in a suggestion system for many years, talks about his experience:

☞ *There are three ways to attain recognition in a large organization. One is to become the leader of a union. The second is to start activities based on work circles. The third is to start making suggestions. I realized that the first two things require somebody else besides you. The only thing that I could do by myself was to make suggestions. I can do the suggestion system in my own way and it depends only on my ability. This is its greatest attraction.*

Since becoming convinced about the suggestion system, A has worked hard toward the goal of winning the company award for the best ideas. Awards are not things you can win by chance, and suggestions don't write themselves. Veteran suggesters who have won awards have done so by setting high goals for themselves, working hard, and carefully studying problem-solving techniques and applications.

Problem Display Board

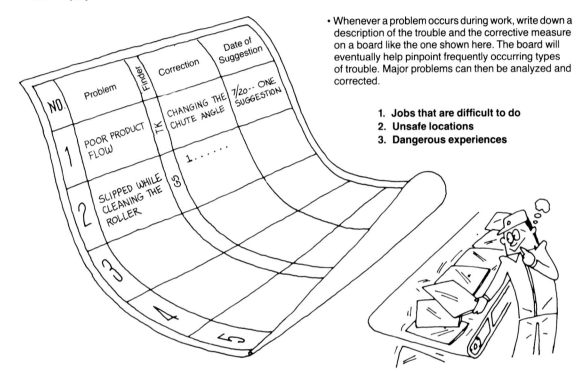

• Whenever a problem occurs during work, write down a description of the trouble and the corrective measure on a board like the one shown here. The board will eventually help pinpoint frequently occurring types of trouble. Major problems can then be analyzed and corrected.

1. **Jobs that are difficult to do**
2. **Unsafe locations**
3. **Dangerous experiences**

Regardless of what you are doing, it is important to set goals. Without goals and the discipline to pursue them, people tend to take the easy way out, writing haphazard ideas when they write at all.

You should set goals for yourself a little higher than your current ability. It is pointless to set goals so high they cannot be achieved, and setting goals entirely within your ability does not lead to either improvement or personal growth. A goal "just over your head" that you have to stretch or climb a little to reach is the most realistic and contributes the most to your personal growth.

Your very first goal is to set a deadline for writing your first suggestion. After you have passed that milestone, the next goal is to work up to the company or shop goal for suggestions per month as soon as possible. After you become comfortable making one suggestion a month, set your goal at making medium- or high-grade suggestions rather than increasing the number of suggestions. Seeking a specific reward for each suggestion is one good way to upgrade the quality of your suggestions.

Display Your Goals on a Graph

Set a goal for each team and for each worker. Each person should write a few words describing his or her ambition for the year.

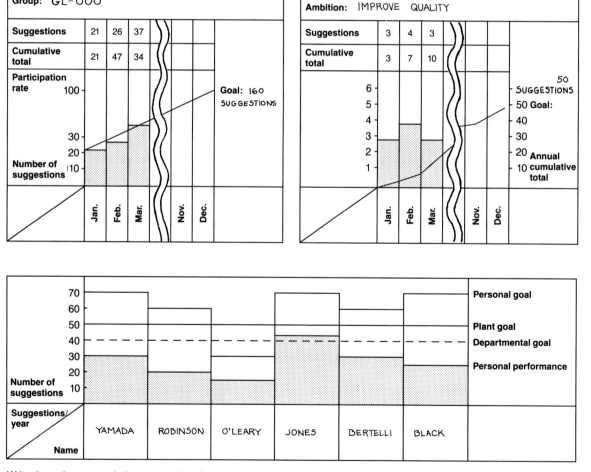

Write down the personal, departmental, and plant goals, as well as the actual performance for each worker so that status of personal suggestion-making is obvious.

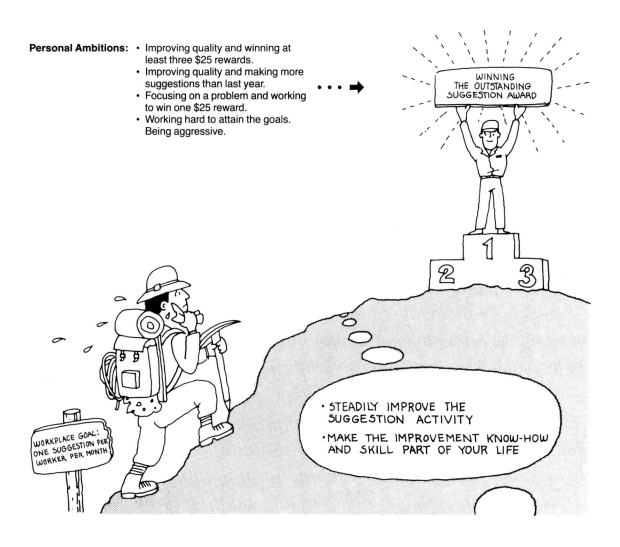

Personal Ambitions:
- Improving quality and winning at least three $25 rewards.
- Improving quality and making more suggestions than last year.
- Focusing on a problem and working to win one $25 reward.
- Working hard to attain the goals. Being aggressive.

WINNING THE OUTSTANDING SUGGESTION AWARD

WORKPLACE GOAL: ONE SUGGESTION PER WORKER PER MONTH

- STEADILY IMPROVE THE SUGGESTION ACTIVITY
- MAKE THE IMPROVEMENT KNOW-HOW AND SKILL PART OF YOUR LIFE

Suggestion Competitions

Once you have set goals for improvement suggestions, make it your personal responsibility to attain them. Plot the performance of individual workers or of whole work areas on a graph, which can be used as a contest. Placing the graph where it is conspicuous inevitably introduces an element of friendly competition. Because the goals are openly declared, the participants want to attain them.

A spirit of competition is embedded in the psyche of every person. Competitiveness is deeply related to ambition. If everyone knows how you're doing, you want to do well — you cannot just sit back and not participate. You don't want to be embarrassed.

As we all know, this is a competitive society. Many people feel that it might be better if competitiveness on the personal level were toned down. For this reason, many companies have systems in which individuals participate in competition on a voluntary basis. In these systems, work areas are the main unit of competition and the performance of individual workers is not disclosed unless they expressly wish it to be.

Tatsuno Matsushita Electric Works held such an "intramural" suggestion competition not long ago. It covered an entire cafeteria wall with a playing board mural depicting the twelve signs of the zodiac, each representing an increasing number of suggestion points. Twenty-three work areas competed with each other, using rocket-shaped markers, starting in Capricorn and moving through the signs to Sagittarius. The goal was to be the first team to cross the Milky Way galaxy.

Points for the competition were calculated according to the following formula:

$$\frac{\text{(Total individual suggestion points)}}{\text{(number of workers)}} \times \frac{\text{(participation rate)}}{2.5}$$

Example of a Suggestion Competition

The Trans-Milky Way Galaxy Race Suggestion Competition

IMPROVEMENT SUGGESTION CAMPAIGN: "USE YOUR WISDOM AND THE GOODS YOU HAVE IN YOUR WORKPLACE."

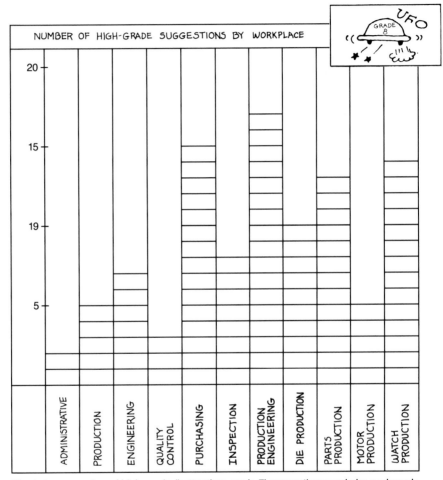

Chart shows number of high-grade (better than grade 7) suggestions made by each work-place. Color-coded labels identifying the specific grade level are placed on the chart as high-grade suggestions are submitted.

The target point value for the groups was 8,776, the number of stars visible to the naked eye. Theme competitions held at Tatsuno Matsushita in other years used different target values (and scoring systems), such as 1,978 for the 1977 "Time Machine Race" (five winning groups), and 800 for the "Home Run Race" (six winning groups).

Tatsuno Matsushita Electric awards a trophy each month to individual workers making the most suggestions or winning the most points and to the workplace with the best suggestion of the month. The winners keep their trophies until the next monthly award is made. A booby prize is also awarded, going to the suggestion group with the worst record, although a weak group that has nevertheless had 100 percent participation that month will be spared. This trophy is a *daruma* figure, a painted roly-poly doll with the eyes left blank (showing blindness to improvement possibilities) and no hands or legs to act with.

Some people may think such a competition is childish. A spirit of fun, however, is necessary for invigorating a voluntary activity.

Self-Improvement

Improvement programs that are carried out haphazardly do not last long. Regardless of how vigorously the program is pushed, the time comes when workers lose interest and there seem to be no more possibilities for improvement. Of course, there are always problems to be solved, but the ability to identify problems becomes dull unless it is continuously refreshed.

Self-improvement is the way to hone your instinct for locating problems. It is accomplished by studying and learning technical information, improvement techniques, and the methods applicable to a particular task. With this knowledge, you will be able to look at a problem from a wider perspective and understand its essence, which will also help you come up with a solution.

Many companies provide opportunities for self-improvement and mutual improvement in the form of in-house or outside training sessions and seminars. After attending such a session, you return to your work area and teach your colleagues about what you have learned.

At the Vacuum Cleaner Division of Matsushita Electric, on days when there is no need for overtime, some foremen and group leaders teach other workers, on a strictly voluntary basis, about value engineering, industrial engineering, and related topics. These courses are very popular because they increase the employees' understanding of the improvement projects.

The Vacuum Cleaner Division stresses improving the skill of its technicians — more than half of the workers engaged in assembly are certified second-grade mill-machine operators.

Useful Learning Programs for the Suggestion System

CTC (creative thinking course): Uses the psychological mechanism to help people tap their own creativity for better ideas.

IE (Industrial engineering): Promotes the planned use of personnel, materials, and equipment using scientific techniques to reduce cost through improvements.

VA (Value analysis): Discloses unnecessary cost in terms of quality, durability, appearance, and use so that cost can be reduced without changing the product's performance level. This is especially helpful for production engineering and purchasing employees.

QC (Quality control): Uses various statistical control techniques to produce the highest quality goods for the least cost under a given set of conditions.

Learning Machining Skills

Having some knowledge about lathes, milling machines, welding, electricity, circuitry, and other machining skills related to your job will allow you to implement your suggestions by making minor modifications yourself.

This machining skill enables the workers to modify and improve their hand tools, jigs, fixtures, and other shop equipment themselves.

Deepening your knowledge and skills not only improves the quality of your suggestions, but also makes improvement activities more interesting and enjoyable.

Making Group Suggestions

Throughout Japan, the number of group suggestions is increasing. Almost all major improvement suggestions — those that yield benefits on the order of several tens or hundreds of million yen ($100,000 to $1,000,000) — are group suggestions. Looked at in another way, the very formation of workers' groups is what allows large-scale suggestions to be developed.

Earlier in the book it was stated that suggestions can be made by one person. It is now time to qualify that statement. Correcting a problem that affects only one worker can be handled as an individual suggestion. A problem that affects the entire workplace or involves other departments, however, usually cannot be solved without the cooperation, collective wisdom, and experience of many workers, even though the problem may have been identified by a single person. Moreover, it often takes another person to spot the defects in a plan that seems very good to the worker who thought it up. This can be done only through a team effort.

Of course, working as a team reduces the reward gained by each worker, and the feeling of accomplishment and independence that comes from working on your own may be diminished. The result that can be accomplished, though, when each member of a group works as hard as possible is quite remarkable.

Compared with individuals, a team of workers can analyze problems at a much deeper level, formulate ideas from a wider perspective, and carry out the plan with a higher level of sophistication.

Group suggestions are likely to become the main vehicle for improvement ideas in the future. The transition from individual suggestions to group suggestions is similar to that observed in the history of science and technology, where the driving force for advancement has shifted from the solitary genius to research teams in organizations.

Benefits of group suggestion-making

- The knowledge and experience of an individual worker tend to be limited and may be biased by preconceptions. A group corrects this imbalance.
- Brainstorming is most effectively done in groups of about ten people. Working over ideas and improving on them in a group can produce a synergistic effect, leading to more ideas and solutions.

- Working as a team allows group members to be responsible for what they do best. This ensures a systematic approach to problem-solving.
- When a problem that affects all the group members is solved by the group, the individual members are usually more satisfied with the solution and therefore tend to use the new method.

Suggestion-Improvement Activities: Personal Experiences

Here is what several workers have said about their experiences with their companies' suggestion systems:

☞ *You must study before you make suggestions. For example, you have to be able to draw blueprints or understand an electrical diagram. You also have to be able to locate problems, and you have to be as curious as a child. This is how I promote the suggestion program.*

In concrete terms, I take notes. I have a notebook in my pocket so I can write down any inspiration I get. Also, I get to the plant early in the morning when my mind is fresh and take a look around the workplace. I look for problems and possibilities for improvement. I've even gone to the toy department of a department store looking for ideas when I ran out of candidates for suggestions.

I also set targets for the year. It is important to make suggestions as you run into problems. But I believe that you cannot make quality suggestions unless you have goals and a deadline, whether it's a year or a month.

Another technique I often use when I run out of suggestions is to divide items into themes such as improving productivity, improving quality, or improving safety. Then, I look for related problems with defects, safety, or whatever, and write suggestions about them. I believe that the important thing with suggestions is to be steady and to continue doing the simple things.

☞ *In the beginning, I wrote suggestions based solely on my experience. However, when I started to run out of things to suggest, I bought books, studied about different materials, machines, and began using this knowledge for greater creativity. I also drew flow-charts on my own to look for waste, inadequacy, or inconsistency. I was always looking for ways to simplify my job.*

I also went to the suggestion system office to study what was being done at other companies. Knowing that there were others who were doing better motivated me when I was facing a mental block. I have the chance to be creative while collecting data and carrying out quality control techniques. Sometimes I feel that the suggestion system is a game I play against myself.

☞ *When I get an idea, I try to write a suggestion that same day. But it is hard to find the time at work, so I have sometimes written suggestions at home, staying up late at night.*

As I began to understand what the suggestion system was all about, I started looking for suggestions with bigger benefits. Whenever the company announced the best suggesters, I told myself I would one day become one of them. One day my supervisor gave me some advice: "Assembly is mainly working with your fingers. It is difficult to improve assembly significantly by improving equipment. It is better to change the work procedure to eliminate small waste. If extensive small wastes are eliminated, a large benefit will be produced."

Since that time, I have been looking for waste, regardless of how trivial it may seem, in the work processes, location of parts, and so on.

☞ *In the beginning, my attitude was to make improvements indiscriminately. I relied mainly on intuition for suggestions. I made many suggestions, but I received only participation awards. I was getting disappointed that I could make only poor suggestions whose benefits were always doubtful prior to implementation.*

I then began thinking of what "creativity in the workplace" meant. I had the chance to take part in a training program called "Workplace and Improvement." I realized I didn't completely understand the objectives of the suggestion system. The training taught me that the important thing was to find out what the workplace needed most and to address that need.

I have changed the way I arrive at suggestions. Now, I divide problems into small segments and combine ideas to come up with an improvement. I pay more attention to how jobs are combined and I try to eliminate defects in quality. Now I have several good suggestions to my credit.

☞ *I feel that the satisfaction from making suggestions depends on where you are in the company — how long you've been there and the stage of growth you have achieved. During my first two or three years in the company, my satisfaction came from receiving a reward. After four or five years, my primary aim was to make my job easier. I was glad that the search for easier ways for doing my job led to suggestions.*

After five years, the important thing for me became the satisfaction of knowing that I was being recognized for making good suggestions. Of course, the reward motivates you to make suggestions.

I have bought books about improvement, notebooks for jotting down ideas, pencils, erasers, and so on, all to improve my ability to make sug-

gestions. I "reinvest" my rewards in things that will help me make better suggestions. There is a snowball effect. Small improvements must be repeated over and over in order to make major suggestions.

My greatest enjoyment now is the energy and youthful drive I experience through improvement activities.

CHAPTER 5

Involving Others in Workplace Improvement

Interpersonal Relationships in the Improvement Activity

Often, a suggestion you think you have written on your own has come about with help from many other people. It may be someone who inspired you or a supervisor or co-worker who advised you. It may be the technical staff who helped you make a prototype or a rival who challenged you to do more. It may be your husband or wife who poured you that cup of tea when you were staying up late writing the suggestion.

Most of the suggestions you write are the products of your interactions with others and responses to their advice. Without them, you probably would not have been able to successfully write the suggestion.

Of course, you have had a similar effect on suggestions made by other people. The suggestion and improvement program are supported by human interaction, which enables the improvement activity to become more active and higher in quality.

Like ripples that expand outward when you throw a stone into a pond, one improvement in a workplace induces further improvements, thus expanding the circle of improvement.

An improvement activity does not stand alone. For the activity to take root in a workplace, all employees must get involved and work together. Only then can the workplace come alive with high-quality suggestions for improvement. On the surface, making improvements may appear to be a purely technical problem. In reality, however, it is tremendously affected by the harmony or absence of harmony in underlying interpersonal relationships.

How can a suggestion program be improved? How can it become more active? These are problems not just for the individual suggesters or the suggestion program office, but for the entire workplace.

The worker-supervisor relationship

- Supervisors can enhance communication with workers by giving advice on how to write suggestions or about the improvement plan.

- From such interaction, the workers learn how the supervisor thinks and get to know him or her as a person.
- From the contents of the suggestions made, the superior gets a feel for the workers' morale and what they think about their jobs.

Peer relationships

- Improvements you suggest increase efficiency and make your co-workers happy. You also benefit from improvements they devise. This breeds a cooperative relationship with your peers.
- Exchanging information on improvement, giving and receiving hints, and mutually extending help during improvement implementation fosters a feeling of camaraderie among co-workers.
- Your colleagues are also your rivals. Competing with your peers improves the quality and the quantity of suggestions.
- Rewards won for suggestions can be used to buy refreshments for meetings or for going out with fellow workers. The suggestions developed with your colleagues strengthen your ties with them. This provides renewed motivation to make more suggestions.

Family relationships

- Most suggestions are written at home because there is usually no time for it at the company. Writing a suggestion gives your family members a chance to help in your endeavor.
- It's a good thing to write suggestions when your children are around. It is a good educational experience for a child to witness the parent working and he or she may even have some fresh and creative ideas to offer.
- Have your husband or wife check a suggestion you have written. If your spouse can understand it, without knowing the intricacies of your workplace, then the suggestion is at least understandable.

The Meaning of "Full Participation"

When you identify a problem needing improvement, it is usually not imperative to correct it that very day. Of course it is better to act as soon as possible, but the improvement can usually wait for another day or two without dire consequences.

Those Who Make Many Suggestions and Those Who Don't

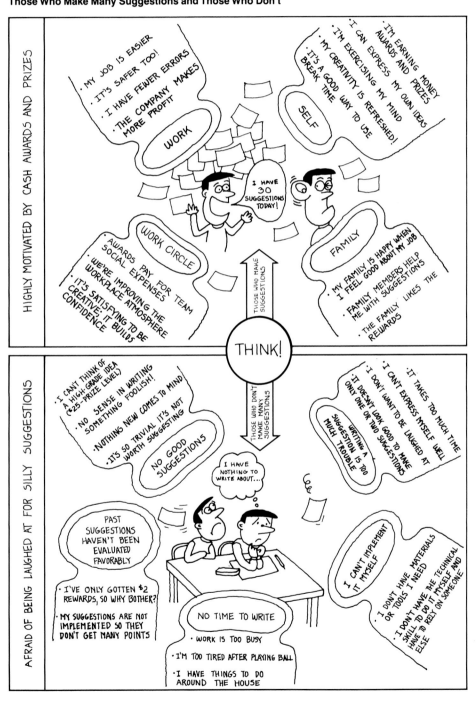

Knowing this usually results in procrastination, especially when you have so much regular work to do. You accept your own excuse, "I am too busy for making improvements." When many people start feeling that way, an atmosphere of procrastination pervades the workplace. Everybody starts feeling that they are too busy.

The situation described above happened with A, a 45-year-old worker. He felt he had no time for making suggestions for improvement. He and two other workers would work the regular hours and overtime just to keep up with the regular workload.

Under the leadership of S, A and the two workers started an improvement project. The improvements enabled the work that previously required three workers to be done by two people, and A's work became much easier. He no longer has to run around just to keep up. He says he never realized that solving deficiencies would make his job so much easier. Now A is a confirmed believer in the suggestion system, and his goal is to win the company's annual award.

Because improvements can usually be put off for a day without any problem, they will not take place unless all workers are highly committed to the program. One worker cannot say that he or she is too busy or that everything is OK as is. "Full participation" is so often stressed because it is essential for breaking through daily procrastination.

Remember that helping and teaching each other and invigorating an improvement program are *everyone's* responsibility.

Suggestion-Making as a Group Effort

The workplace is the classroom for improvement. In T's workplace, employees meet every morning to discuss strategies for improvement.

"I get too busy when I have to assemble Product C. Because of that I had to stop the line twice yesterday. I wonder if there is any way to improve the situation?"

"Please show us how you are doing it at this time."

T demonstrates how she actually performs the job.

"Well, I think you're walking too much during assembly. If

Ideas for Suggestion Meetings

Schedule suggestion meetings

Once a week, twice a month or whatever, you should decide when you will meet to write suggestions as a group. It is usually hard for everyone to find time to write suggestions during work. You can avoid that complaint by setting aside time for it. You can also exchange information about suggestion writing techniques at these meetings.

Demonstrate your job for improvement pointers

Demonstrate in front of everyone what each of you do or how you perform your job and let others point out unnecessary motion.

Collect ideas from everyone about the suggestion each of you intends to make

Discuss how the suggestions themselves can be improved. Through this activity the quality of suggestions is refined and everyone can learn how to make better suggestions.

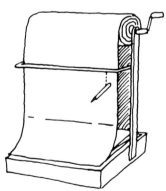

Everyone jots down problems as they notice them

At the Mizushima Plant of Mitsubishi Motors, workers use a roll of scrap computer paper in the workplace so that anyone can jot down anything he or she notices during the day. At the meeting everyone thinks of solutions to the problems raised that way. (The paper is rolled out using a handle.)

Use outside sources

At some point you may feel there is no longer anything left to improve in your workplace. It is important, then, to collect information from outside your own work area. Learn from improvement cases of other departments and companies and follow their examples when you can. Information you gain through exchange meetings with other circles, in-house training, and outside seminars should be shared with all the members in the group.

you could stretch your body a little, you could perform the job without walking so much."

The group members take turns performing their standardized procedures in front of each other and discuss whether there is wasted motion. By doing this, they see many unnecessary movements they never noticed individually.

During the morning meeting, the group sometimes writes suggestions on the blackboard and discusses them.

"I understand what you intend to do, but something isn't clear to me. What is the difference between before and after the improvement?"

"There are too many words. Why don't you use a drawing to explain the suggestion more understandably?"

"Just a moment. If you implement this suggestion, it could cause inconvenience to the next process. I suggest you check it with them first."

Through the discussion, a simple idea presented by one worker is developed into a well-thought-out suggestion. It becomes more specific and its quality improves.

It is really effective to provide employees with this kind of opportunity since it can teach them how to analyze problems, work out their own ideas, and report the suggestion. Even new employees feel less shy showing their suggestions to their co-workers first — it's not so intimidating as writing one up and turning it in to the supervisor. Through group improvement sessions, everyone can understand what the others are doing and work to create a common vision of their work. The workplace is the classroom for improvement — it has to be!

Learning from Past Improvement Examples

Often, an old idea triggers a new idea. This is why learning from someone else's idea is a fundamental method of formulating suggestions.

When an idea becomes a commercial product, copying it usually violates laws or contractual agreements. Transferring ideas within a single company is a different matter. Copying and adapting something to another situation is one way to improve and add value to excellent ideas.

How far an idea is improved and adapted determines the depth of an improvement suggestion program. If individual improvements are never adapted to other situations, the suggestion program may enjoy temporary success but it won't be able to sustain any momentum.

If you run out of suggestions, look at the improvements made by others. You may see things you never noticed before and get many ideas you can borrow.

When a suggestion is made, it becomes everyone's property. An idea should therefore be used to stimulate more ideas. It is helpful to examine all suggestions for their adaptability and to create a handbook of sample improvements. Another useful sharing technique is to make a bulletin board display for the latest example of a good suggestion, attaching before-and-after photos to highlight the improvement. One workplace did this on a team basis, which publicized the improvements accomplished by the team.

Displaying examples of improvements

- Purpose:
  a) To expand the application of a suggestion
  b) To stimulate development of new ideas
  c) To stimulate competition among groups and workers

d) To learn from other workers' examples how to organize ideas and write suggestions

▪ Method:
a) All suggestions are mounted on a display board as they are submitted.
b) If suggestions must be selectively displayed, choose not only those receiving high scores but also those with a high degree of adaptability, innovation, and good writing skills.
c) Instead of just displaying them, publish the suggestions as a handbook or manual so that they can be studied in group sessions.

Exhibiting Past Improvement Examples

At Kansai Electric Company, a conference room in the head office has been made into an exhibit area for 30 model suggestions. The review committee selected them for adaptability and easy comprehension from several hundred items that had won everything from the President's Award to the "grade four" score. Examples include illumination meters, current leakage experimenting equipment, and easy-to-read safety manuals (see pages 94-95). When you look at each item, you can imagine how each item was improvised at the workplace. Other interesting examples include a vacuum cleaner for cleaning fluorescent lamps, a contraption for removing kites tangled in electrical lines, and a buzzer to tell you your refrigerator is open.

This display takes place every year from October to January. After the exhibits are shown at the head office, the display travels from one branch office to another (over 200 sites), showing primarily local exhibits. The president and other executives, as well as more than half of all workers, visit the display to get hints for developing their own ideas.

Production floor workers get a lot of satisfaction when the exhibit publicizes their names and ideas throughout the company. All exhibits use actual samples, unless they are too large. For example, a model shows a new method for constructing electrical line towers, and a cutaway display shows the inside of an oil strainer. A video program in the exhibit room shows improvements that can be understood only by viewing. The improvements are described in the film by the suggesters themselves.

"One Improvement a Day" Program

The "one improvement a day" program is launched from time to time in a company to encourage employee involvement through generation of simple, basic ideas from each worker. Every worker is strongly urged to make one suggestion every day.

At Aisin Seiki, a Toyota subsidiary that makes brakes and transmissions, this program is in effect for 20 days each year. During this period, every worker carries a pocket notepad with "one improvement a day" printed at the top. When an improvement is made, he or she writes it up on a page and tears that page off. Examples of such notes include: "I picked up and put back trash that had fallen from a trash can," or "I put away the used cups that were left in the conference room." Some actions may not qualify as genuine "improvements," but during this campaign they are accepted. Workers must nevertheless be very alert in order to make an improvement every day. It is amazing how fast cups and ashtrays are removed at the end of the next meeting after the first "improvement"!

The torn-off notebook pages are displayed on a bulletin board as shown in the figure on page 97. The pages overlap

	1977	1978	1979
Program period	January-March	February	February
Number of days	57	20	20
Number of improvement examples	18,600	7,790	9,200
Number of improvements per worker per day	0.81	0.93	1.11

Note: More than 420 employees are involved in the program

A Bird's-eye View of the Suggestion Exhibit at Kansai Electric

Thirty superior suggestions representing the different branch offices are shown for three days at the exhibit site. The exhibit moves on to 200 different branch offices. In all, 280 items are exhibited.

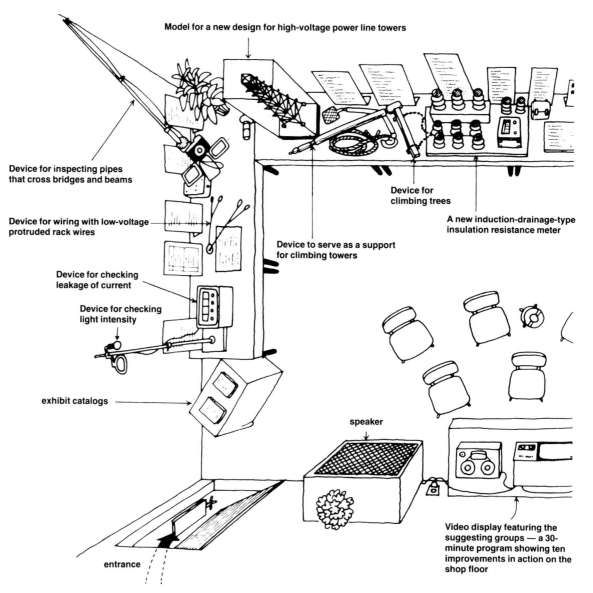

Model for a new design for high-voltage power line towers

Device for inspecting pipes that cross bridges and beams

Device for wiring with low-voltage protruded rack wires

Device for checking leakage of current

Device for checking light intensity

exhibit catalogs

Device for climbing trees

A new induction-drainage-type insulation resistance meter

Device to serve as a support for climbing towers

speaker

Video display featuring the suggesting groups — a 30-minute program showing ten improvements in action on the shop floor

entrance

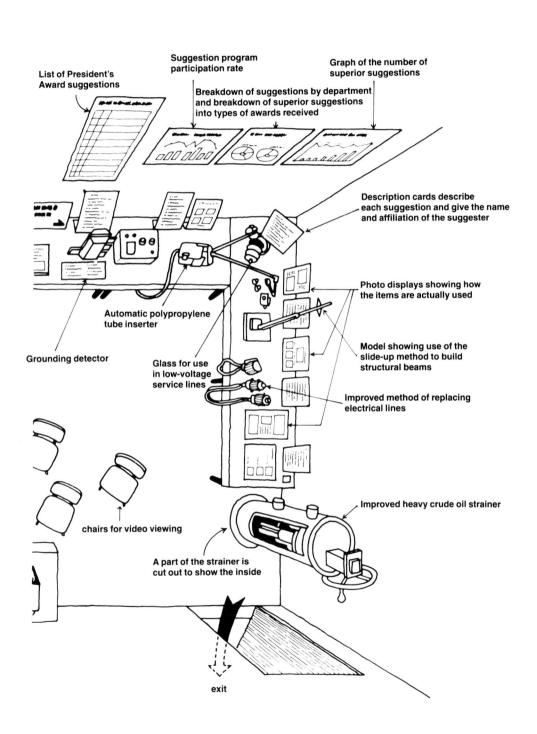

List of President's Award suggestions

Suggestion program participation rate

Graph of the number of superior suggestions

Breakdown of suggestions by department and breakdown of superior suggestions into types of awards received

Description cards describe each suggestion and give the name and affiliation of the suggester

Photo displays showing how the items are actually used

Automatic polypropylene tube inserter

Model showing use of the slide-up method to build structural beams

Grounding detector

Glass for use in low-voltage service lines

Improved method of replacing electrical lines

Improved heavy crude oil strainer

chairs for video viewing

A part of the strainer is cut out to show the inside

exit

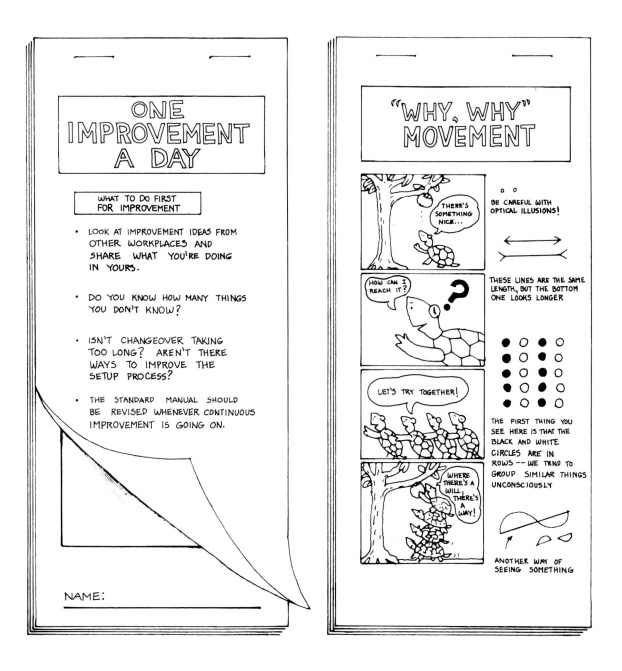

"One improvement a day" notepad

The compact notepad has improvement pointers written and clear directions for using it. Each of the 30 or so pages has sections titled "I found this problem" or "I improved it this way." Workers write up at least one improvement each day, tear the page from the notepad, and post it on the bulletin board. The cartoon takes off from the fable of the tortoise and the hare to show the importance of steady work.

Increased Employee Creativity

14-fold increase in three years

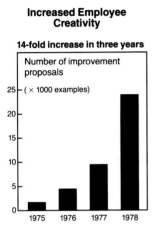

slightly, automatically producing a bar graph of the number of suggestions per worker. Moreover, it becomes readily apparent who isn't making a suggestion a day, motivating people to submit their improvements.

Because actual improvements made by fellow workers are displayed, interest in the program increases and communication improves. This serves as a springboard for finding the next problem.

The premise of the "one improvement a day" program is so elementary that you might say it is like kindergarten for an improvement suggestion program. However, the knowledge and the experience become the property of each worker, and the program creates the appropriate climate for producing creative suggestions.

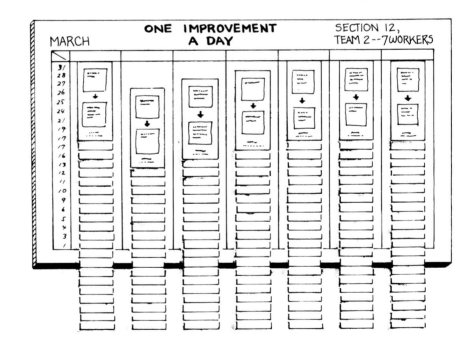

• Each group has its own bulletin board. The pages from the notebook are publicly posted there, with the overlapping pages automatically creating a bar chart.

Using Suggestion Reward Money Effectively

Rewards are the greatest attraction of the suggestion system. Everyone thinks about what he or she could do with the money. Most workers know in advance how they have to spend their paycheck. A cash award for a suggestion is a usually a bonus that can be spent more freely. This section may therefore be unnecessary. However, we would just like to introduce the readers to some constructive ways suggestion reward money has been used.

A typical use is to pool some of the reward money as a group, jointly managing the fund. With group suggestions, many teams pool the entire reward. Even with individual suggestions, five- or ten-dollar rewards given for the lowest category of suggestions can be pooled at the workplace.

The pooled fund can be used to finance work group activities, buy refreshments for meetings, and purchase equipment such as calculators or stop watches for use in the improvement activity. The fund may also pay for parties, trips, and other events to enhance fellowship among the workers.

In carrying out an improvement activity, many work groups rely heavily on the technical staff for information and advice. K notes that he often uses his rewards to take members of the technical staff out for a beer to get to know them better. Winning a cash reward is not merely an end in itself, but also the means to promote further cooperation and creative activity.

The CTT group of Matsushita Electric reports that a winner of the President's Award donated the ¥1 million ($4,367) to a charitable group. This is a unique use of a reward for the benefit of society.

Expanding the Horizon of Your Ideas

An exotically dressed woman appears on the stage, sitting on a sheet of glass carried by four men wearing turbans. The magician throws a sheet of cloth over the woman, says the magic words, and pulls back the cloth. She is no longer there. The trick

Ways to Use Suggestion Reward Money

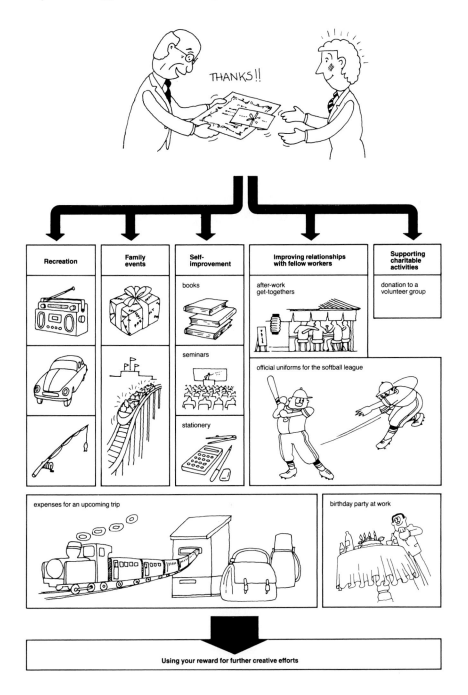

is that one of the four men is actually a hollow figure through which she escapes out of sight.

Once you know the trick, there is no mystery. However, to develop new ideas, you must look at things from different angles, make the effort to acquire stimulating information, and take the risk of trial and error.

As you continue to use your creativity in improvement activity, you begin to enjoy the act of creativity itself. It becomes enjoyable to be creative not only in work but in all aspects of your life. The purpose of Toyota's "Idea Olympic" and Nisshin Steel Company's "Idea Concours" is to provide a forum outside the framework of "work" to stimulate the development of creative ideas and products.

At the "Idea Concours" at Nisshin Steel, literature about inventions is displayed along with samples, such as flat lenses, paper that dissolves in water, and a contraption for creating cube-shaped boiled eggs. When you look at these inventions, they stimulate you to think of uses for them.

Attending an event such as this makes you realize that people are truly thinking creatures. Each invention is so ingenious that you want to own it and use it. You get the feeling that the inventors probably enjoyed themselves very much while coming up with the invention. Work improvement is not the only way to express your creativity. Why don't you try expanding your horizon of ideas?

Involving Others in Creativity and Idea Generation: Activities of the Toyota GI Club

(This section was contributed by Tsuyoshi Bando, president of the Toyota GI Club.)

The Toyota GI Club is a voluntary work circle. "GI" stands for "good idea." The club is composed mainly of people who have won an annual award in the company's creativity suggestion system. The purpose of the club is to realize Toyota's motto of "Good Products, Good Thinking" by sharing the joy of learning and the joy of creating.

Expand Your Ideas!

- **Some exhibits shown at the Toyota Idea Olympic**

Automatic dashed-line drafter:
Dashed lines must often be drawn on blueprints. However, it is difficult to draw proportionally spaced dashed lines, leading someone to devise this automatic dashed-line drafter. A cam moves the pencil up and down to create the dashes.

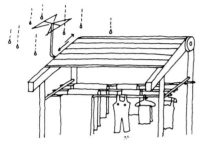

Rain-shielded clothes-drying platform:
A water-sensitive antenna automatically trips a switch to move a shield over the platform when it rains. When the antenna dries up, the switch is tripped again, this time to open the shield.

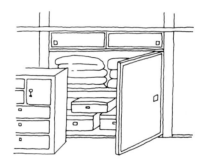

Universal door:
Can be used both as a sliding door and as a swinging door. The door opens all the way so large items can easily be pulled out or put away.

- **Some exhibits shown at the Nisshin Steel Kure Plant Idea Concours**

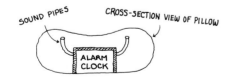

Pillow with built-in alarm clock:
Devised by a father whose children were consistently late for school. The pipes direct the alarm sound toward the sleeper's ears.

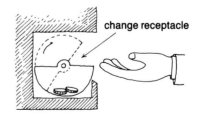

Improved vending machine change receptacle:
Receptacle rotates so that the change falls into your palm.

The 1972 winners of the Gold Award visited some of the plants of the other Toyota companies. Because the winners came from throughout the company, I did not know many of them. However, we had the chance to talk about our jobs and our creative efforts, and we developed a feeling of camaraderie. I enjoyed everything about the trip.

Three or four months after the trip, I happened to run into some of the other participants. We talked about the trip and decided to reconvene the group again. Because six members attended the party, we called the group the "The Gang of Six." We met frequently at members' homes for meals and drinks paid for by a party fee.

Eventually the club was renamed the "Good Idea Club" as our membership expanded. Eighteen winners of the 1972 and 1973 Gold Awards met in June 1974. Those who couldn't attend the party requested that we meet again the next year so that they could take part in it. This led to the founding of the GI Club.

Until about 1976, the GI Club was primarily a social club. In between the drinking and the laughing, we'd talk about improvements, but we came to feel we were wasting an opportunity to combine our individual suggestions into a larger benefit.

As a result, we created subcommittees at our workplaces. The intention was for the individual club members to act as leaders in raising the level of creativity at each workplace to encourage the development of other superior suggesters.

As a result of our activities, there are now ten subcommittees with over 400 members. In some workplaces subcommittees are just being started. The monthly fee is about one dollar. We are always trying to reduce our operating costs and sometimes receive financial aid from the suggestion system office.

The figure on page 103 shows the organizational structure of the GI Club and its activities. In a nutshell, the purpose is to promote friendship and mutual improvement among the members and to contribute to the development of the company through creative activities.

In 1978, we issued our first club newsletter. A monthly club magazine called *GI Times* was also started. Each subcommittee is responsible for holding a sample improvement announcement

Organization of the GI Club

The club office is housed within
the Creativity Improvement Office.
Members must be employees of Toyota.

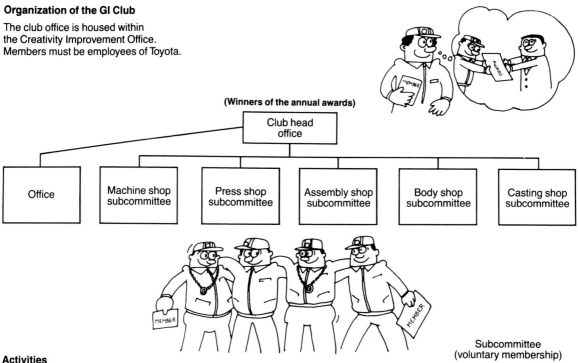

(Winners of the annual awards)

Club head office

| Office | Machine shop subcommittee | Press shop subcommittee | Assembly shop subcommittee | Body shop subcommittee | Casting shop subcommittee |

Subcommittee
(voluntary membership)

Activities

Holding discussions and visiting
other Toyota group companies

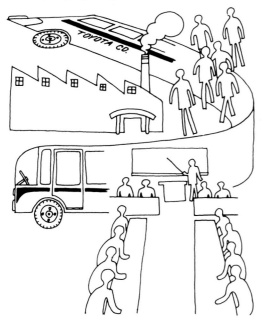

Club objectives

• Adapting and using superior suggestions
• Holding seminars for invigorating the suggestion activity
• Holding seminars and events to promote interaction
  among members
• Developing friends with whom to think about creativity

session on a monthly rotating basis. The subcommittees also sponsor creativity study sessions once a week after work. These sessions are open to non-members, and the suggestion system promotion office provides refreshments.

The club offers classes on creativity. We prepare educational material and are actively involved in training of new recruits and on-the-job training. The suggestion program office sends us reports on suggestions made, and we try to encourage those who show ability to become superior suggesters if they put in a little more effort. We have also offered classes on value analysis and zen practice, and we often sponsor overnight trips to nurture friendship among workers.

It's been a number of years since the club was started. The club is now receiving some attention in the company, and the company newspaper has published articles about our activities. This has given us confidence and further motivation. Possibly because of that, 26 of the 32 workers who were distinguished suggesters for three years in a row were members of the GI Club.

Distinguished suggesters are selected from workplaces that have active subcommittees, and most workplaces that are honored for their suggestion activity have an active subcommittee. We believe this is because the club-related activities improve the attitudes of club members in the workplace. We also believe that the club gets supervisors interested in developing workers with high creativity.

The GI Club has grown over the last few years, with the help of our supervisors, the suggestion system office, and the members. Our accomplishments cannot be expressed simply in terms of numbers. We want to cherish not only the improvements that creativity allows us to make but also the intangible benefits such as the joy of working and the satisfaction of improving.

CHAPTER 6

How to Guide a Suggestion System

Concerns of Leaders

Full participation is the most fundamental condition for the success of any suggestion program. However, there is a precondition for full participation to occur: the presence of committed leaders who serve as the core of the activity.

Think back to how you began your personal involvement in the suggestion program. You probably had questions such as, "What is a suggestion?" or "How should suggestions be written?" The simple act of eliminating waste in the workplace must have seemed very difficult. It undoubtedly took a lot of effort to overcome the initial difficulties. You might have had an easier time of it if someone had helped you with timely advice. You might have begun to write good suggestions much earlier.

The primary role of foremen and work circle leaders is to provide advice and promote the suggestion system. The leaders' enthusiasm — or lack of it — significantly affects the number of suggestions coming in, the quality of the suggestions, and the overall participation of people in the workplace.

A "leader" is a person who can make his or her own suggestions but who also provides assistance and guidance to the less experienced. Because leaders also make suggestions, their advice is convincing. With a fresh memory of what it was like to be a newcomer to the suggestion system, the leader can offer timely advice to novices. The success of the suggestion system hinges on the commitment and enthusiasm the leaders have for their supportive role.

Getting Workers to Write Their First Suggestions

When a person is working wholeheartedly at a task, he or she is usually making improvements without knowing it. Making improvements is almost instinctive. The only difference between people may be that some make improvements unconsciously, others with more awareness of what they are doing.

Providing guidance about making suggestions is basically nothing more than helping a person realize his or her innate ability to make improvements and teaching the person how to pack-

Guidance Hints for Different Experience Levels

Level	Goal	Problems	Countermeasures
New worker	One suggestion per month	• Don't know what to write. • Don't know how to write.	• Teach the worker why suggestions are necessary. (Why must quality and efficiency be improved? Why must cost be reduced? Why must production quantity, safety, and so on be increased?) • Ask what inconveniences he or she has experienced in working. • Make an improvement in the worker's job and write the improvement on a suggestion form as an example. Review the suggestion form with the worker. • Starting with the third or the fourth suggestion, have your worker and a more experienced person work together to identify a problem and suggest an improvement. • Evaluate highly the first suggestion independently written by the worker. If problems are found, point them out carefully.
3-4 years' experience	Three suggestions per month	• The required number of suggestions is barely being met. • No progress is seen. • The person is working hard, but the quality does not improve.	• Tell the worker to observe things closely — any waste is a candidate for improvement. • Point out problems that will lend themselves to improvement. • Solve a problem together and show the worker how to look for problems, analyze them, and develop solutions. • The leader should share his or her own suggestion and teach the worker how to write and summarize suggestions until the worker fully understands. • Let the worker understand that the suggestions are necessary not because they are required but because they concern problems that affect the workers themselves.
Junior supervisor grade	Five suggestions per month; improved suggestion quality.	• Lacks enthusiasm. • The idea is good but poorly written. • The worker is not finding satisfaction in suggesting and improving.	• Introduce the worker to books about developing creativity and making improvements to promote self-improvement. • Provide the worker with a chance to meet workers from different departments or companies who are also involved in making improvements. • Give the worker examples of good suggestions for study. • Set up a competition among workers of like ability. • Challenge the worker with a major goal, such as winning a corporate award.

PROVIDE INFORMATION,
TAKE INITIATIVE,
GIVE ADVICE AND HINTS,
APPROACH GRADUALLY

I'M BECOMING MOTIVATED!!

age each improvement as an official suggestion. You don't need to guide the person through every detail, but you must do more than present a target number of suggestions to the worker, pat him or her on the back, and say, "You're on your own."

Newcomers need to experience success. Most people make suggestion-making more difficult than it needs to be. This becomes a psychological barrier to making suggestions. It is important for workers to realize that it's something they really can do.

To give the new worker the experience of success, the leader may need to help the worker locate a problem in the job, improve the problem, and present the improvement as a suggestion in the worker's name. The next time, the worker can copy the first suggestion. Of course, the first few suggestions will be less than perfect, but as long as the suggestions satisfy the minimum requirements, the worker should be properly recognized for the effort.

Tell the worker that he or she has done well and made a good suggestion. Remember how you felt when you made your first suggestion. Be encouraging!

It's a long road to the well-made suggestion. You should not expect an employee to start out doing everything perfectly, from identifying the problem to writing a thoughtful presentation. An employee should be praised at first simply for writing up his or her own suggestion.

Approaching People Who Don't Write Suggestions

"Working is not easy. On the production floor, my movement is planned to the last second as if I were a part of a machine. If you are in sales, you have to be nice to the customers whether you want to or not. We have to show respect to our boss. We can't take a rest when we want to. Now, on top of everything else, we're asked to write suggestions."

"A suggestion system is supposed to be voluntary, but if you don't make suggestions your fellow workers wonder what's the matter with you. Making suggestions is almost mandatory, even though I'm already doing my work well and don't have time to write them."

Are You Discouraging Workers Without Thinking?

- Everybody knows that.
- Your suggestion has never been tried. It's probably impossible.
- I tried it before and I know it won't work.
- This isn't up-to-date enough.
- It won't work the way you planned it.
- There are already too many suggestions. I'll look at your suggestion when I have time.
- Let's talk about it some other day.
- Let's wait and see what happens.
- Why do you want to change it? It's working well.
- There are rules. This won't work.
- The technical staff will say your idea won't work.
- Your idea is too farfetched. The boss won't OK it.
- We can't use your idea at this company.
- That might work in Japan, but not in the U.S.
- Life is more complicated than that.
- You probably won't understand it.
- It's a good idea, but we don't have the budget.
- That will create problems later.
- Don't come to me for advice.
- What *is* this suggestion? Can't you make it a little better?

THINK WITH THE WORKERS

These are things you might hear from employees who don't make suggestions. When they present such arguments, the supervisor will probably not know what to say. There isn't much to argue about with them; what the people are saying is basically true.

But does the worker truly mean what he or she is saying? When everyone else is making suggestions, not making any is probably harder on the worker than sitting down and writing one out.

Most likely, the worker has not had the opportunity to make a suggestion before. He or she may not know what to write about or how to write up an improvement idea. People tend to think they can forget about writing once they leave school. Writing is a very tedious task for some people. Many workers are embarrassed about their writing ability or their penmanship.

To convince someone like this to write a suggestion, the leader must empathize with the worker. Logical arguments are not the answer — the leader must understand what the worker is feeling and offer a helping hand. This kind of caring inspires the worker and nurtures creativity.

One Supervisor's Experience in Guiding Suggestion Writing

A, age 57, was an experienced machinist. He would not take part in any other job, however, and was a generally uncooperative person. He would stay away from work if he felt like it and he didn't listen to others. He never wrote a single suggestion.

In the past, A had taught Murata, now a foreman, about machining. When A was transferred to his team, Murata asked A why he did not make any suggestions. A said: "Murata, look at it this way. I'm retiring in two or three years. Why should I want to do something as bothersome as writing a suggestion?"

Murata did not expect to easily convince A to write suggestions. He made up his mind, though, to spend one year persuading A to make suggestions. He began having frank discussions with A, convinced that the suggestion system was the only way to make him feel some camaraderie with his fellow workers.

Murata went drinking with A, and invited him to mahjongg games. He discovered that A was a very sincere person with quite a bit of technical knowledge. He also learned that A was disillusioned with his repetitive work and that a large part of his uncooperativeness had its roots in this disillusionment.

Murata told A: "You're really overlooking an opportunity here. Why don't you leave behind something for the company in the time before you retire? It will probably be a memory you will remember the rest of your life. What you can do on your own is to write suggestions and to shoot for an award for your ideas."

After seven months of encouragement, A started writing suggestions like a new man. He soon became the best suggester in his team. He made his own improvement plans and started working twice as hard. And his relationship with the other workers improved. The memory of his success with A is one of Murata's most satisfying experiences with the suggestion system.

Guiding Suggestion Writing Is the Supervisor's Job

The leader's job is to make the workers' jobs easier to perform, safer, and more enjoyable. In doing this, the leader promotes efficiency and contributes to good management of the company.

In this age of rapid technological progress, however, the production floor workers are sometimes forgotten. Workers may feel they have become human robots, stuck in repetitive activity. The workplace becomes a monotonous place and loses its vitality and morale.

A workplace should be a living organism that responds to what is happening inside and outside the company. New problems emerge there all the time, and the leader and workers can solve them through a cooperative effort in the suggestion system. This is one way to expand the workers' abilities, introduce an element of newness every day, and breathe fresh air into the workplace.

The role of leaders in an improvement activity isn't just to promote the suggestion system but to invigorate the workplace, strengthening the morale of the workers and helping them develop their abilities. This is a challenge for the leaders as well as for their subordinates.

Changing A's Attitude about Making Suggestions

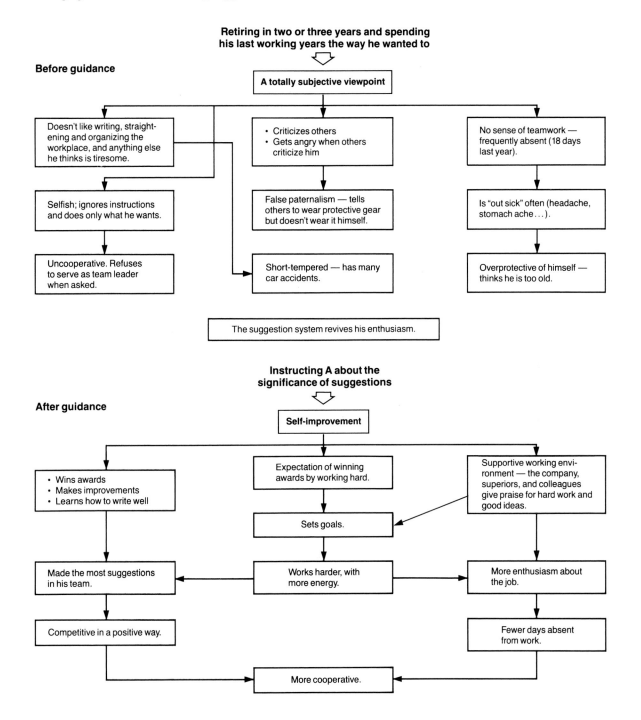

Before guidance

Retiring in two or three years and spending
his last working years the way he wanted to

A totally subjective viewpoint

Doesn't like writing, straightening and organizing the workplace, and anything else he thinks is tiresome.

- Criticizes others
- Gets angry when others criticize him

No sense of teamwork — frequently absent (18 days last year).

Selfish; ignores instructions and does only what he wants.

False paternalism — tells others to wear protective gear but doesn't wear it himself.

Is "out sick" often (headache, stomach ache . . .).

Uncooperative. Refuses to serve as team leader when asked.

Short-tempered — has many car accidents.

Overprotective of himself — thinks he is too old.

The suggestion system revives his enthusiasm.

After guidance

Instructing A about the
significance of suggestions

Self-improvement

- Wins awards
- Makes improvements
- Learns how to write well

Expectation of winning awards by working hard.

Supportive working environment — the company, superiors, and colleagues give praise for hard work and good ideas.

Sets goals.

Made the most suggestions in his team.

Works harder, with more energy.

More enthusiasm about the job.

Competitive in a positive way.

Fewer days absent from work.

More cooperative.

Providing guidance to workers regarding the suggestion system is a way to ensure that no worker is left behind in the improvement effort. The leader's guidance enables workers to take a critical look at the operations they perform every day and teaches them to enjoy the delight of creating.

Making suggestions can indeed be difficult and tiresome sometimes. However, there is satisfaction in the effort as well. With good guidance from their leader, workers can learn to enjoy the challenges and the feeling of achievement from conquering a tough problem. The leader should have confidence in this!

A leader can't just tell the workers to "make suggestions" without making a personal commitment to the improvement activity. The leader's enthusiasm and active participation sparks the workers to make a committed effort in the improvement program; nothing will really change in the workplace without it.

Guidance to Improve the Quality of Suggestions

A worker once complained that when he read other people's suggestions, he felt the workers were just blowing their own horns. This realization, he said, discouraged him from making suggestions. What he meant was that the suggestions were little more than routine improvements. Why, he wondered, should he pat himself on the back by formally writing these things down as official suggestions?

It's unfortunate that the worker saw it this way. Why didn't his supervisor think to encourage him to tackle problems he felt were more meaningful? It is important, of course, to start out making a lot of suggestions to improve minor problems around the workplace. If this approach is continued too long, however, workers will lose interest. Making many suggestions may mean more reward money, but there should be other motivation to take on bigger challenges.

In describing a suggestion system, the number of suggestions is usually stressed, with emphasis on a continuously increasing target number. Of course, minor improvements are important to this number. But there's more to a suggestion system than just numbers. Once the workers become familiar with the suggestion

The Most Common Reason for Not Making a Suggestion Is the Fear of Having Ideas Ridiculed

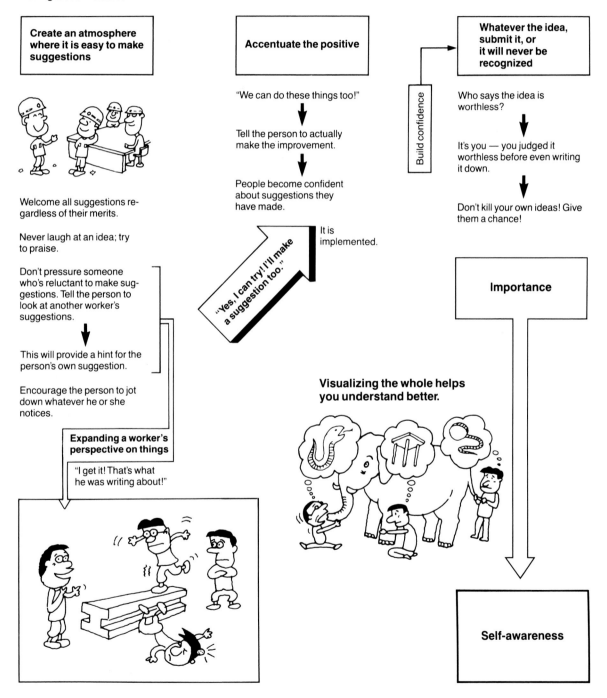

Create an atmosphere where it is easy to make suggestions

Welcome all suggestions regardless of their merits.

Never laugh at an idea; try to praise.

Don't pressure someone who's reluctant to make suggestions. Tell the person to look at another worker's suggestions.

This will provide a hint for the person's own suggestion.

Encourage the person to jot down whatever he or she notices.

Expanding a worker's perspective on things

"I get it! That's what he was writing about!"

Accentuate the positive

"We can do these things too!"

Tell the person to actually make the improvement.

People become confident about suggestions they have made.

It is implemented.

"Yes, I can try! I'll make a suggestion too."

Build confidence

Whatever the idea, submit it, or it will never be recognized

Who says the idea is worthless?

It's you — you judged it worthless before even writing it down.

Don't kill your own ideas! Give them a chance!

Importance

Visualizing the whole helps you understand better.

Self-awareness

Tips for Leaders in the First Stage

- Set a good example by making suggestions.
- Cast a critical eye over the jobs where problems occur often. Listen well to workers and other supervisors. Understand what needs to be improved.
- Every chance you get, emphasize to your workers and colleagues how important it is to make suggestions, and encourage them to do so.
- Provide advice to help workers and colleagues prepare suggestions.
- Examine each suggestion carefully. When something is unclear, ask the suggester to clarify it. Point out poor writing and better ways of expressing the idea as you notice them.
- Regardless of the magnitude of the suggestion, try to examine it with an eye toward implementing it. Give the suggester hints how it can be implemented, if necessary.

From subordinates and colleagues:

- Accept the cooperation and help that make the job more effective.
- Gain respect and trust by making them think in a constructive manner.

For subordinates and colleagues:

- Provide the chance to make their jobs easier and more efficient.
- Give them satisfaction and pride in seeing their suggestions implemented.
- Develop a habit of critically evaluating their job activities.
- Express appreciation to their leader, whose advice and assistance helped them win rewards and recognition.

Before demanding suggestions from workers, cultivate the proper environment for their ideas to grow in.

system, the leaders must provide the advice and assistance they need to create and attain new goals for improvement. For instance, leaders can set out specific areas of improvement for the workers to take on, coordinate group suggestion-making, and challenge the workers to try for company awards for their ideas.

Individual personality and ability determine a worker's educational needs. The needs of the workplace also dictate what management would like the workers to learn. The leader is in the position to know both the worker's and management's needs and to make a judgment as to what is best.

This is not easy to do. An educational program must be well thought out, however. A high level of commitment is necessary for the suggestion system to become an effective tool for human development in the workplace.

Tips for Leaders in the Second Stage

1	Once suggestions are being made voluntarily, you need only provide hints. Forcing the leader's will on workers who have developed to this level will only blunt their creativity.
2	Make sure the workers realize that merely making a suggestion does not complete the task. Encourage them to view the problem from different perspectives and consider what implementation will require. This will increase their understanding of the improvement system.
3	Suggest useful books to assist workers in formulating their improvement ideas. Have workers participate in training seminars or challenge a new task. Expose them to as many stimuli as possible. Don't let them lose enthusiasm — remind them that the finish line is still a long way away, with much to be done before they get there.
4	Have the workers set personal goals, distinct from the company or workplace goals. Encourage them and provide the advice, help, and information they need in reaching the goal.

Suggestion-Writing Methods: Personal Examples

☞ *At my workplace, the examiners and our supervisors offer tips on how we can improve our suggestions in order to win more cash awards or get better results. The entire workplace is involved in the suggestion system and it's proving to be very effective. A suggestion system that was forced on the workers would not have lasted long. The important thing is creating the atmosphere that makes people want to make suggestions voluntarily.*

☞ *I notice that many suggestions miss the mark by a little bit. I often hear people say that having to write a suggestion is too cumbersome. I think the truth is that the person does not know how to express himself or how to write, so I help him focus his thoughts. For example, in a morning meeting, I write A's idea on a blackboard and ask each participant what could be done to improve the suggestion. The timing of advice is also important. It seems that giving advice during our 10:00 A.M. meeting is the most effective. This is probably because the 10:00 A.M. meeting takes place after the workers have already been at work for two hours, and their minds are sharpest at that time. This is when physical and mental fatigue is probably the least.*

☞ *Before the workers in my group submit their suggestions, I look through them and make sure they are understandable. I ask them to clarify ambiguous points. That way when the evaluation committee asks me to explain a point, I can usually provide a detailed description. This has a favorable effect on the evaluation. By deepening the ties between my subordinates and myself, we produce suggestions that the examiners can understand better.*

☞ *I tell my subordinates, "Just go write something. I don't care what." However, words alone aren't enough, so I try to create an atmosphere conducive to suggestion-making. For example, during lunch break I play badminton and try to take part in recreational events outside the work environment. This cultivates a friendly relationship with my workers. Then when I say, "Go write some suggestion," or "Why don't you write about this," it is more effective. When someone doesn't write suggestions because he feels he has nothing to write about, we talk about it heart-to-heart. Sometimes, I give the person a memo showing how I'd write it.*

☞ *The leader must show the effects of the improvement to the worker. Just saying it won't make the worker a believer. I think any improvement, no matter how trivial, must be carried out as soon as possible. I believe it's a*

good thing for the leader to propose additional ideas to make the suggestion better.

☞ *To get workers interested in the suggestion system, you have to find an example of waste and ask what they would do to make it better. The idea is to use on-the-job training to eliminate unnecessary motion, increase efficiency, and make jobs easier. By solving a problem as a group, workers gain satisfaction and confidence in knowing the benefits of their ideas and become interested in the results of their suggestions. Once suggestions start coming, you can set a target, whether it's one a month or two a month. I have the workers keep track of the number of their suggestions. This automatically increases the number of suggestions they make. The supervisor's job is to provide appropriate opportunities for making suggestions about the workplace.*

☞ *I try to implement all improvement suggestions I receive from my subordinates. If a suggestion is difficult to implement, I ask the worker to consider using a different approach. I do this to trigger new ways of thinking. A suggestion system will succeed on its own if the workers believe the supervisors are interested in their suggestions and ideas. I have achieved success by encouraging my workers to make suggestions, implementing them, submitting the improvements as implemented suggestions, and then having the workers suggest new ideas, starting it all over again.*

How One Work Circle Got Excited about Suggestion Writing

(This section was contributed by Michiro Waga, Waga Circle, Second Maintenance Section, Kariya Plant, Aisin Seiki.)

The argument

The foreman at our workplace was not a very strong-willed man. So we took advantage of this, and we'd ignore the work rules and try to do as little as possible to get by.

One day, we heard a rumor that our company's organizational structure was changing and that the foreman was to be replaced by a new man with the reputation of being a real hard-nose. We didn't want to give up the comfortable arrangement we had, so we hatched a plan to boycott the new foreman so we could get rid of him.

When he assumed the post, the new foreman appealed to us to change our bad reputation. When we heard him say this, we laughed to ourselves, knowing the plans we had for him. The workplace morale was very bad, and the foreman seemed to be hopelessly isolated from us workers.

State of the Workplace under the Old Foreman

Workers talk about a boycott

The New Foreman Arrives

One day we were very busy and the new foreman was working beside us on the production floor. Because of his presence, we were working hard, but because we had been so used to taking it easy, our hard work was hardly enough. After a while, one of the team leaders asked the foreman to give us a rest. The foreman yelled at us, calling us "idiots" and telling us we had to finish what we had been doing and couldn't just stop. This sparked a verbal confrontation. One guy said the foreman had no right to call us names, that we weren't going to cooperate with him, and that things were better without him.

To our surprise, the foreman apologized for yelling at us when we were doing our best. He was very understanding. We had heard of his reputation so his sympathetic side surprised us. I learned once again that, for better or for worse, people do not always live up to their reputation.

A heart-to-heart discussion

Through such episodes, we gradually got to know each other and we were warming up to each other. One day, a worker suggested using an upcoming three-day vacation for a camping and fishing trip.

AN ARGUMENT HAPPENED ONE DAY!

LET'S TAKE A REST

YOU'RE CRAZY! FINISH WHAT YOU'RE DOING!

CHANCE FOR A BOYCOTT!

We had been tired, both physically and emotionally, from the recent changes, so everyone agreed to the idea. But we didn't know of a place where we could camp and fish. One worker said, "Maybe the foreman knows one. He's a fishing fanatic." We made the guy who had the idea go and ask the foreman. He

Drinking and talking...

to learn more about each other outside the work environment.

Dinner from the fish caught together

didn't know what to expect, but he went and asked the foreman if he knew of a good spot. The foreman liked the idea — and asked if he could come along. So, we all went together to Sakatejima in Mie Prefecture.

We fished during the day, and at night drank and ate what we had caught. We forgot about work and laughed, sang, and talked. The foreman loosened up and started talking about all the good things about his former workplace. He said, "The workers in my last shop were motivated. They made enough suggestions on their own. I never had to goad them. Compared with them, this shop is the pits!"

Hearing this, the workers began to get a little angry. After a while, we decided to show him that we could do as well as anyone else. We said that we would write suggestions too.

Later on, we started regretting that we had promised on the spur of the moment to make suggestions. We'd stare at the suggestion forms, but we didn't use them.

After several months passed this way, I saw the foreman writing a suggestion himself. He had gotten fed up with us, who never lived up to our promises to write suggestions and had finally decided to persuade us by action. I felt bad.

We held a meeting, and there I suggested that we write suggestions too and not be outdone by the foreman. There were two views in the meeting; those who agreed to write suggestions and those who said they'd never do so. I tried but failed to convince the three who were adamantly against writing suggestions.

I had just been chosen the leader of a QC circle and even though I did not have any good ideas, I decided to do the best I could. I tried but failed to convince the three to try writing suggestions. When I had a heart-to-heart talk with C, he said, "My penmanship and writing ability are poor. I'm not a good writer, so I can't make suggestions." E said, "I don't have anything to write about." G said, "I don't care what anyone else says — I just don't want to make suggestions!"

I realized that the suggestion system would never take off in our shop without the support of these three workers, so I decided to give them my personal attention.

The Leader's Difficulties at the Beginning of Suggestion Activity

Something finally clicks

I borrowed a handbook for C that showed examples of suggestions from the plant office and from other workplaces. We looked through the handbook and tried to write a suggestion. But C was never comfortable doing it, so I had his best friend join us and the three of us wrote a suggestion in a very relaxed atmosphere.

For E, who complained that he didn't have anything to write about, I suggested that he look at things from a different perspective than the routine angle. He wrote a few suggestions after this.

I had the hardest time with G. I asked myself, "How can I pique the interest of someone who just doesn't care about the suggestion system?" I didn't come up with any answer, but one day I yelled at him. I berated him for not making any suggestion when everyone else was trying so hard. This only made him more adamant, while C and E were slowly making an effort to write suggestions. G remained unmoved. I realized that yelling was definitely the wrong approach, so I decided to go out for a drink with him.

We started talking about our families and memories of the past. During the conversation, G began to reveal his true feelings. He said, "I don't what to make suggestions without substance, suggestions that are nothing more than changing the shape or motion of something." I told him, "That's fine. But you shouldn't be too concerned about making *good* suggestions. Good suggestions can result from making many small suggestions."

Finally, G lightened up and promised me he would try writing a suggestion. I felt and hoped that this would invigorate the suggestion activity of my circle.

Becoming a distinguished suggester

We were surprised one day when F came in second place in the annual suggestion contest and won the President's Award. We didn't know there was even a contest. Also on the list of our plant's five workers with the most suggestions were B, who belonged to my work circle, and K, also from my workplace. The difference between B and F, the award winner, was minimal. Their success inspired our entire workplace.

Encouraging the Three Workers

F Receives Second Prize in the Plant

After that day, we worked hard at making suggestions, promising ourselves that someone from our workplace would win the first and the second places next year. We devoted our lunch hours to writing suggestions in order to become distinguished suggesters. During the suggestion system promotion month, we got the competitive spirit running by setting up a blackboard to show the number of suggestions made.

However, during one particular promotion month, 19 of our suggestions were rejected. When I asked the foreman why, he replied that suggestions presented more than six months after implementation are not accepted. Also, there were three identical suggestions.

My circle members and I weren't satisfied with this answer. We could understand the rejection of identical suggestions, but no one ever told us that suggestions older than six months were not acceptable. This bit of news put a damper on what had become a motivated circle. During the month after this, we did not make one suggestion.

The foreman noticed this and asked me why our circle wasn't making suggestions. I told him we were still recovering from the shock of the rejections. He told me we were taking it all wrong. We should think about why our suggestions were rejected, he said, and I wasn't being a very good leader.

I was again shocked and couldn't forget his words even when I went home. Finally, it came to me that many suggestions were rejected because we didn't know the rules of the game, and the identical suggestions resulted from poor communication within our circle.

Goal: To become distinguished suggesters

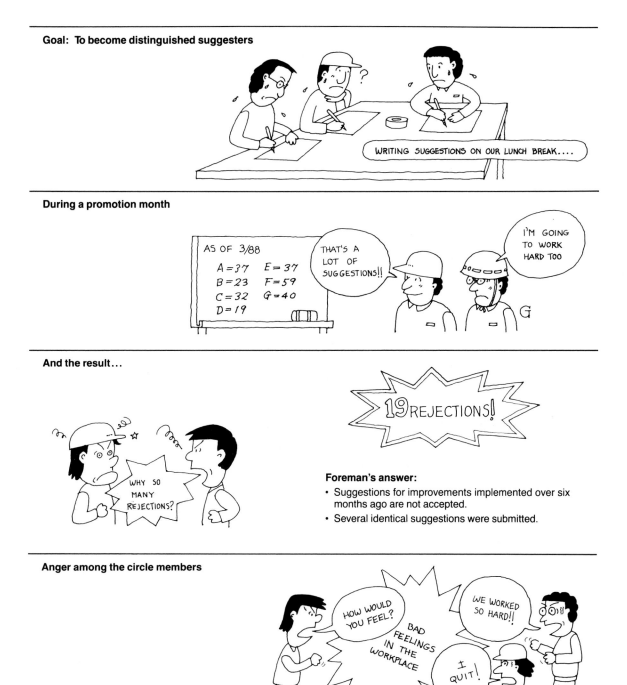

During a promotion month

And the result...

Foreman's answer:
- Suggestions for improvements implemented over six months ago are not accepted.
- Several identical suggestions were submitted.

Anger among the circle members

I realized that I had gone along with my circle members just so they would like me. I felt my circle would become unproductive if I kept this up. I resolved to change my direction — to become more aggressive and start producing ideas.

Starting from scratch

I called a meeting of our circle in order to start anew using the two following principles:

- To create a circle whose members can discuss things freely, study, and cooperate together.
- To set goals and aggressively promote the improvement activity.

I pointed out to the members of my circle how we always quit whenever we faced some difficulty and that was why we were seen as a stupid circle — we were regressing. I also carefully explained why our suggestions had been rejected and showed that there was no one but ourselves to blame.

The circle members all resolved to try again to redeem ourselves. We agreed that:

- We would use the suggestion rewards as the work circle fee so that all circle members would make suggestions.
- We would levy fines for those who do not achieve the goals.
- The 10th, 20th, and 30th of each month would be designated as "suggestion days" when suggestions must be submitted. This was done to keep us constantly aware of suggestion-making.

As the leader of the circle, I worked to promote teamwork by sponsoring discussion meetings over tea. I prepared group documents and assigned a role to each member to instill a feeling of participation. Since we all had difficulty in planning improvements because of the sophisticated equipment that was used in our workplace, we held technical training classes for the circle members.

To foster a feeling of camaraderie that would extend beyond just the workplace, I also started recreational activities that involved friends and family members and took an active part in weddings, births, and other festive events.

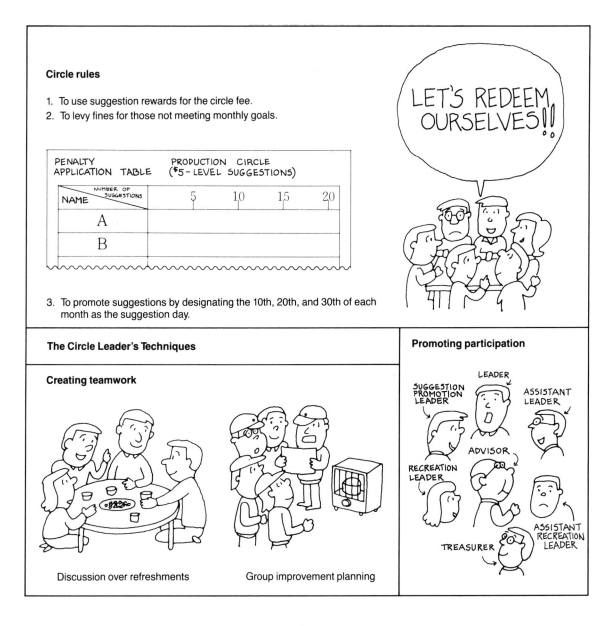

Circle rules

1. To use suggestion rewards for the circle fee.
2. To levy fines for those not meeting monthly goals.

PENALTY APPLICATION TABLE   PRODUCTION CIRCLE ($5-LEVEL SUGGESTIONS)

NAME / NUMBER OF SUGGESTIONS	5	10	15	20
A				
B				

3. To promote suggestions by designating the 10th, 20th, and 30th of each month as the suggestion day.

LET'S REDEEM OURSELVES!!

The Circle Leader's Techniques

Creating teamwork

Discussion over refreshments   Group improvement planning

Promoting participation

SUGGESTION PROMOTION LEADER   LEADER   ASSISTANT LEADER   ADVISOR   RECREATION LEADER   ASSISTANT RECREATION LEADER   TREASURER

Results of team activity

These activities led to increased teamwork, and our suggestion activity improved yearly. In the first year we made 178 suggestions. Within five years this increased to 2,217 suggestions, a

Setting High Goals

twelve-fold increase. During that period we occupied first and second place. One year, when the competition format pitted one circle against another, our circle came in first in the factory. During the past several years, the number of grade-two technicians, electricians, high-voltage electrical technicians, and other licensed workers in the circle increased dramatically.

When the time comes for the annual year-end parties, we receive gifts from the production floor workers, thanking us for our daily efforts. We gratefully accept the gifts, which remind us that our efforts are being recognized and make us pledge to work even harder.

It has been several years since the easy foreman was replaced by the hard-nosed foreman. Although it was a difficult road, these last years have convinced me that nothing is impossible if you try hard enough.

CHAPTER 7

Two-Way Communication via the Suggestion System

Suggestions as a Barometer of Workers' Attitudes
Two-Way Communication
Concerns of the Suggestion Evaluators
How to Use Evaluation Standards
Evaluation as an Educational Opportunity

Suggestions as a Barometer of Workers' Attitudes

When Japanese suggestion systems were still imitating the suggestion systems that originated in the United States, Japanese middle managers felt their jobs would be superfluous if regular workers were allowed to make suggestions directly to the company. The managers were understandably anxious about what the workers were suggesting. They had the impression that a large number of suggestions indicated a large number of problems and reflected poor management by them. There were undoubtedly some managers who wanted to say, "Don't make too many suggestions. If you have the time, you should be working."

This type of attitude about the suggestion system is long gone. Managers now consider the act of suggesting to be an indication of the worker's enthusiasm for his or her job. It is also understood that workers cannot spot problems and make improvement suggestions unless the workplace is managed competently. The suggestion system is not an activity in which only peripheral workers participate; it is integrally related to those in management.

Management should welcome and take pride in workers who are making constructive suggestions. Suggestions indicate workers who are serious about their work, are making an effort to increase their efficiency, and are transforming the workplace into an easier and safer place.

In other words, the quantity of suggestions made is a barometer of the enthusiasm of the workers, and the quality of the suggestions is a barometer of management's skill in nurturing this enthusiasm.

Two-Way Communication

There aren't any managers who still believe they can create a successful suggestion program by making an announcement, putting up a few suggestion boxes, and waiting. Things just don't work that way.

From the discussion so far, we hope the readers realize that a suggestion activity requires tremendous effort and commit-

Responsibilities of Supervisors

Establishing policies

- Establishing departmental policies for suggestion activity
- Setting goals for suggestion activity, considering the departmental conditons and the opinions of their subordinates
- Determining suggestion topics to solve specific problems existing in their department
- Modifying the system and the evaluation/rewarding criteria in response to the status of suggestion activity, or soliciting views regarding such modification

Evaluation

- Evaluating the suggestions that fall in their areas of responsibility

Rewarding

- Giving rewards based on an established system

Training

- Continuously reminding the workers about the need for their suggestions
- Providing improvement hints and advice to promotion leaders, and implementing other OJT programs
- Giving feedback to the production floors about things noticed during evaluation
- Providing education to improve the workers' skill and knowledge about improvement
- Encouraging workers to take part in seminars, exchanges, and other improvement-related events both in and outside the company to expand their viewpoints

Implementation

- Making the arrangements necessary to implement the suggestions
- Giving advice and helping workers implement their own improvements
- Promoting the adaptation and use of suggestions made in other departments

Promoting the suggestion system

- Planning and assisting with contests and campaigns to motivate the workers
- Using the suggestion system as much as possible for ideas during business planning for their departments

ment from the supervisors and the suggestion system staff. Regardless of the talent of individual workers, as a group most employees tend to be hesitant and slow to act on their own. Most suggestion systems are voluntary activities. Such programs, even with financial incentives, will not succeed without a lot of management effort and support.

Encouraging a person to share his or her ideas carries much more weight than ordering someone to write a report. Because suggestion activity is voluntary, the workers don't just jump into it, and management must use whatever method and expend whatever effort it takes to obtain the worker's trust and participation.

On the surface, a suggestion system seems to be a one-way communication from the workers to management. But a closer observation will show, hidden in the background, another channel running from management to the workers. That channel is used for evaluating and implementing the suggestions, giving rewards, giving directions, soliciting suggestions, encouraging and educating the workers, providing competitive incentives, and making sure that the goals are properly managed.

The suggestion activity is therefore a full-fledged two-way communication activity, with both directions equally important. Management gives direction to workers' creative thinking and receives valuable ideas and information in return.

Concerns of the Suggestion Evaluators

In the flow of information from management to the workers, the notice giving evaluation results for a suggestion is one of the most important communications a worker receives. This is what concerns the suggester most. All suggesters are anxious to open the letter and read it. Their hopes go up and down with the strength of the evaluation and the comments of the evaluators. Typical comments include:

"Accepted. Your effort to correct even the slightest problem has paid off. Please keep up your good work."

"Other improvements are also possible. Please reevaluate your suggestion."

"Not accepted. We regret to inform you that your suggestion is too costly considering the benefits. However, your perception of the _____ problem is unique. Why don't you analyze the situation using the _____ approach? We believe good results will occur."

Most companies pay a cash reward for improvement suggestions that are submitted. The evaluation is an important process in this system. Workers must have trust in the evaluators. Without this trust, a suggestion activity will fail. Each evaluator must remember this.

There are two components to the trust the suggester has or should have. One is that the evaluation will be done in a fair manner. In other words, the judgment of the evaluators must be correct and unbiased, with consideration for the overall good of the business.

The second part of the workers' trust is that the evaluators are working to help each suggester to improve. The evaluation must offer help and encouragement and point out possible directions to the suggester.

Fulfilling these two expectations is not easy. However, it is essential that the evaluators at least try to fulfill these expectations.

How to Use Evaluation Standards

Suggestion evaluation can be broadly defined as the process of assessing suggestions in light of management's wishes. Since "management's wishes" is probably too ambiguous to be fair and useful, a set of evaluation criteria must be established. The guidelines used for ascertaining the value of a suggestion are called "evaluation standards."

An evaluation standard generally has three elements: benefits, effort, and creativity. More factors are added if necessary, and the factors are weighted accordingly, creating a single evaluation standard table that reflects the wishes of management.

Tangible benefits, such as reduced cost or time, can be measured quantitatively, making subjective evaluation unnecessary. But intangible benefits, such as improvement in quality, safety, environment, or interpersonal relations, are harder to measure. Measuring effort and creativity is also difficult.

Suggestion Activity Is a Two-Way Communication

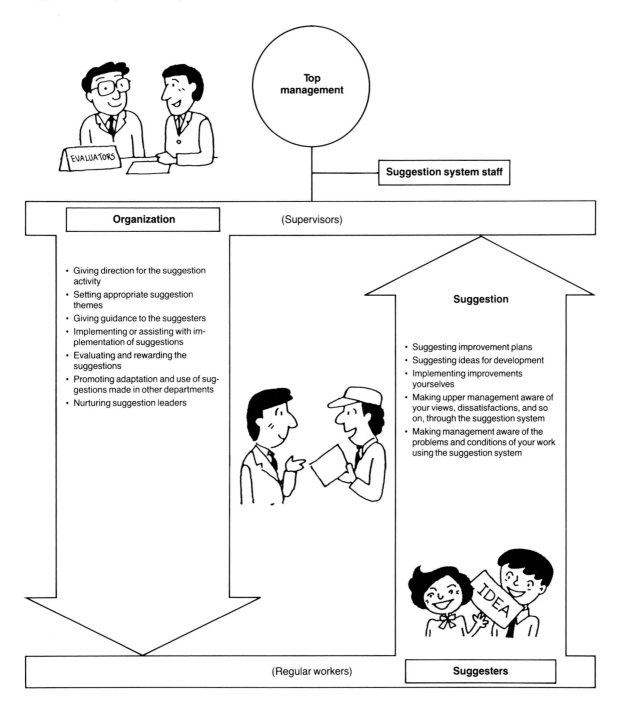

Points to Remember in Evaluating Suggestions

1.	Not all suggestions can be fairly evaluated while sitting at your desk. Questions about a suggestion should be resolved by going to the production floor and discussing the question with the suggester or the worker's supervisor. Be patient and find out what the worker is trying to say. The ideal is to show the suggester at that time how to write better.
2.	A suggestion that looks superficially bad or outdated may still contain good ideas. Study each suggestion well. Don't jump to conclusions.
3.	Be generous with first-time suggesters to build up their confidence. If at all possible, the evaluator should try to accept the suggestion, making personal additions to the suggestion if necessary.
4.	With workers experienced in suggestion-making, evaluate their suggestions and motivate them to challenge higher goals. For example, ask them to re-submit their suggestion after making specific improvements.
5.	Consider the level of the suggester when evaluating his or her suggestion. If you underestimate a person's ability, he or she will not grow. If you expect too much, you will discourage the worker's creativity. Even in discussions with suggesters, the evaluators must try to tailor their comments so that they are understood.
6.	Evaluators have the experience of having once been serious suggesters. But make sure that your past success does not get in the way.
7.	Suggesters are anxious to hear the evaluation result. Evaluate suggestions promptly. If a delay is unavoidable, notify the suggester of the reason for it.
8.	If possible, verbally notify the suggester of the evaluation result. Make sure to add a few words of encouragement, especially if the idea is not accepted. When providing a written notice, always add some comment instead of just the result.
9.	A suggestion is the product of the suggester and his or her supervisor and leader. Do not forget to compliment all of them for their efforts.

> **Evaluation** means making sure that the suggester's ideas are given a chance to grow.
> **Replying** means talking in depth with the suggester.

For example, the spectrum of "creativity" evaluation may range from "completely unique" to "mere imitation." The evaluation of "effort" may range from "has overcome major difficulties" to "no evidence of effort." The evaluator must select a phrase that corresponds to his or her feeling. Regardless of the number of phrases, though, it's not always possible to correctly and mechanically select a phrase that accurately reflects the degree of effort or creativity. At best, a range of options is presented to the evaluator, who must subjectively select one.

It is most important for evaluators to develop the correct evaluation skill. He or she must know what the management is looking for and keep that in mind while evaluating many suggestions about many different types of problems. The evaluator must have a feel for the suggestion trend. Without a feel for the suggestion effort as a whole, it will be very difficult to assess specific evaluations correctly.

Evaluation as an Educational Opportunity

For a suggestion system to take root in a workplace and to improve in quality, the supervisors must have a supportive attitude. It is when the suggester is watching the supervisors evaluate a suggestion that he or she feels most acutely whether or not the supervisor is supportive.

It is important to make a fair evaluation. However, it is equally if not more important to use the evaluation as a tool to encourage the suggester and to make sure that he or she keeps reaching higher. The evaluator should think of ways to tell workers when their suggestions are not accepted without discouraging them. In fact, evaluators should think of how to use the opportunity to motivate the workers to do more. If a worker is showing little progress, think of how this can be corrected. One way of accomplishing these things is to look for ideas in each suggestion that could be expanded into a better suggestion.

Look for the positive points, not the negative, when evaluating suggestions. There is no "perfect" idea. Be sure to tell the suggester what you notice. Don't hesitate to make the effort to go to see the suggester. If you can't do that, remember to add a warm comment on the evaluation sheet.

One veteran suggester said: "The worst evaluator from the worker's viewpoint is the one who is slow in evaluating suggestions. The second worst is the one who doesn't write any comment. If your suggestion comes back with a 'Rejected' stamp and nothing else, you feel like you will never make a suggestion again."

Example of a Typical Evaluation Standard

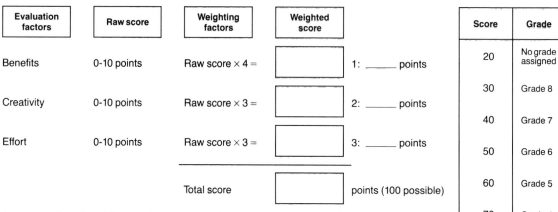

Evaluation factors	Raw score	Weighting factors	Weighted score		
Benefits	0-10 points	Raw score × 4 =		1: _____ points	
Creativity	0-10 points	Raw score × 3 =		2: _____ points	
Effort	0-10 points	Raw score × 3 =		3: _____ points	
		Total score		points (100 possible)	

Score	Grade
20	No grade assigned
30	Grade 8
40	Grade 7
50	Grade 6
60	Grade 5
70	Grade 4
80	Grade 3
90	Grade 2
100	Grade 1

A raw score is assigned for each factor. The raw score is multiplied by a weighting factor to figure the weighted score. The total score is then added up. From the total score, a grade that serves as a basis for rewards is assigned.

By Serving as an Evaluator:

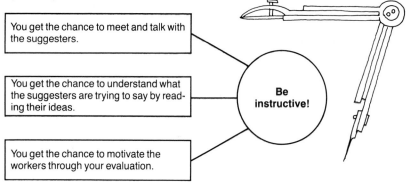

You get the chance to meet and talk with the suggesters.

You get the chance to understand what the suggesters are trying to say by reading their ideas.

You get the chance to motivate the workers through your evaluation.

Be instructive!

Improve Your Evaluation Skills

Learn the improvement condition:	Go to the production floor and look at the improvement condition. Know what the actual improvement methods are as well as how the workers are being given guidance.
Study examples of improvements:	Read as many examples of good suggestions as you can. Study how they were evaluated and compare the method to yours.
Expand the application of the suggestions:	Exchange widely applicable suggestions with other evaluators to spread the benefits of the ideas.

How to Handle Some Typical Situations

---

1. When a new employee makes his first suggestion

This is the first of many suggestions he will make during his career. First, congratulate him for making the suggestion, period. Then, congratulate him for whatever is good in the suggestion. Build up his confidence. Remind him that his supervisor and his leader had helped him in writing the suggestion. Remember to recognize them for their efforts also.

2. When a suggestion is no more than a complaint or an opinion

Discuss the complaint or the opinion with the worker and her immediate supervisor. While making sure not to discourage the worker from making more suggestions, point out the difference between a complaint and a suggestion. Remind her that suggestions must be accompanied by a solution to a problem.

3. When a similar suggestion has already been made

Do not reject the suggestion outright. Tell the suggester that a similar suggestion had been made. Give him hints for improvement and ask him to revise and re-submit the suggestion.

4. When a worker clearly did not write the suggestion by herself

Discuss the problem with her immediate supervisor. Often, the supervisor has written up the suggestion because the suggester didn't know how or because the supervisor wanted to motivate that person. Advise the supervisor how she can motivate the suggester to write the next suggestion herself.

5. When the suggester is clearly dividing a single idea into many suggestions to increase the number of suggestions

Make the suggester understand that consolidating the different suggestions into a whole results in a better suggestion. Teach him that a quality suggestion is more important than sheer quantity.

6. When a suggester cannot win an award regardless of her great effort

Advise her of how she could improve her writing to make the suggestion proposals. Advise her immediate supervisor how the worker can learn more about improvement techniques and skills.

7. When a problem is too large for the worker to solve himself

This problem occurs before implementation. Consult the related departments or senior evaluators. Don't make a hasty decision. Ask the technical staff for guidance in evaluating the suggestion, and get the permission of the appropriate authorities.

A Collection of Suggestion System Slogans

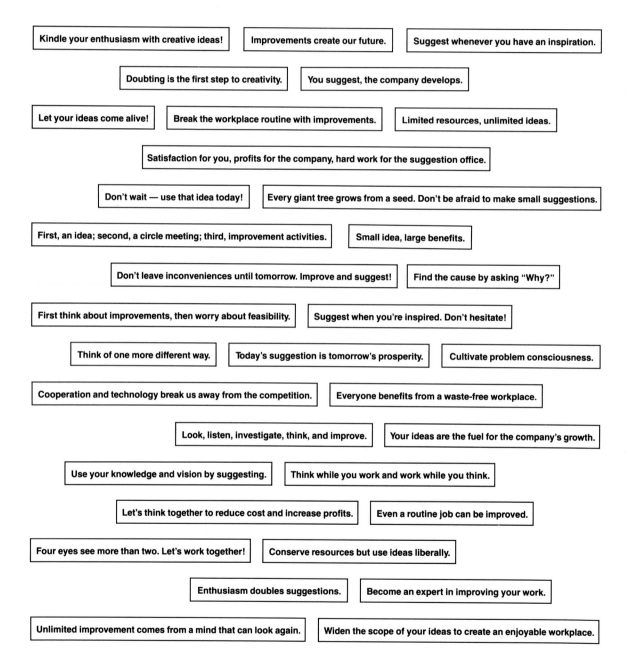

Kindle your enthusiasm with creative ideas!

Improvements create our future.

Suggest whenever you have an inspiration.

Doubting is the first step to creativity.

You suggest, the company develops.

Let your ideas come alive!

Break the workplace routine with improvements.

Limited resources, unlimited ideas.

Satisfaction for you, profits for the company, hard work for the suggestion office.

Don't wait — use that idea today!

Every giant tree grows from a seed. Don't be afraid to make small suggestions.

First, an idea; second, a circle meeting; third, improvement activities.

Small idea, large benefits.

Don't leave inconveniences until tomorrow. Improve and suggest!

Find the cause by asking "Why?"

First think about improvements, then worry about feasibility.

Suggest when you're inspired. Don't hesitate!

Think of one more different way.

Today's suggestion is tomorrow's prosperity.

Cultivate problem consciousness.

Cooperation and technology break us away from the competition.

Everyone benefits from a waste-free workplace.

Look, listen, investigate, think, and improve.

Your ideas are the fuel for the company's growth.

Use your knowledge and vision by suggesting.

Think while you work and work while you think.

Let's think together to reduce cost and increase profits.

Even a routine job can be improved.

Four eyes see more than two. Let's work together!

Conserve resources but use ideas liberally.

Enthusiasm doubles suggestions.

Become an expert in improving your work.

Unlimited improvement comes from a mind that can look again.

Widen the scope of your ideas to create an enjoyable workplace.

(Compiled from Japan Human Relations Association surveys)

CHAPTER 8

Identifying Potential Improvements through Examples

There are no easy rules for finding problems. If all operations of a company are improvable, problems should be found anywhere. It may seem contradictory to try to discuss specific methods for identifying potential improvements. In fact, it is impossible, since every situation is unique. It is a good thing, however, to review what our predecessors have done and to learn techniques that can assist us in finding and solving problems.

The examples given in this chapter are intended to do just that. They are meant to be hints to the reader. A more detailed analysis of problem-finding methods is left to books dealing with the specific subject matter.

Improvements in Work Methods

Identifying Potential Improvements

It is best to start out improving small problems around you. The first step is to find waste, inadequacy, and inconsistency in your job and your motions.

Identifying candidates for improvement in work methods

- Is there a different way of doing it?
- Can you oversee a greater number of machines?
- Can the time now spent waiting be used for some other purpose?
- Can a single motion replace several motions?
- Can it be installed or removed with one motion?
- Can a troublesome set-up be eliminated?
- Can a machine do a manual task?
- Can a process be shortened or eliminated?
- Can a rhythmical motion be used?
- Can a more comfortable posture be used?
- Are both hands being used?
- Can your foot be used?
- How about changing the position of handles, switches, and levers?

Principles of Motion Economy

A man named Frank Gilbreth developed what he called the "principles of motion economy." Gilbreth's motion study has been developed and refined to a fine discipline. This technique shows some of the common methods for improving motion.

Reducing the number of basic motions

- Eliminate unnecessary motion.
- Reduce eye movement.
- Combine two or more motions.
- Place materials and tools in a fixed position in front of the worker.
- Arrange materials and tools in the order in which they are used.
- Use containers that allow materials and parts to be grabbed easily.
- Move in the same direction that the equipment moves.
- Combine two or more tools into one.
- Use a mechanism that allows tools to be tightened with a minimal amount of movement.

Moving at the same time

- Both hands should start and stop moving at the same time.
- Move both hands at the same time in a symmetrical motion but in opposite directions.
- Improve efficiency by using the feet when working with both hands.
- Position the materials, tools, and machine so that both hands can move at the same time.
- Use a holding tool to hold something for a long time.
- Devise tools that allow both hands to move at the same time.

Reducing the distance of motion

- Minimize the distance of movement.
- Perform motions in the optimum body position.
- Make the work area the smallest size that is not restrictive.
- Use gravity-driven tools to move materials.
- Design machines to be operated at the optimum body position.

Making motion comfortable

- Alter or eliminate jobs requiring force, unnatural posture, or excessive care.
- Use gravity or some other force to produce motion.
- Use inertia or repulsion to produce motion.
- Plan the direction of motion to be natural and smoothly changed.
- Make the work position a comfortable height.
- Use tools and guides to restrict the path of motion.
- Design grips to be grabbed easily.
- Design tools so that position can be aligned from a comfortable viewing position.

**Principles of
Motion Economy**

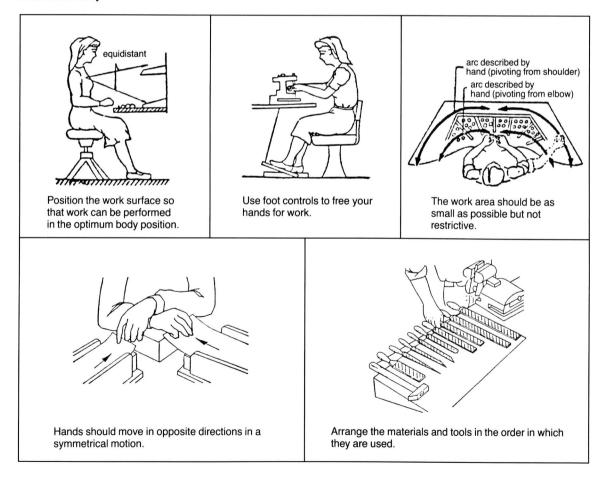

Position the work surface so that work can be performed in the optimum body position.

Use foot controls to free your hands for work.

The work area should be as small as possible but not restrictive.

arc described by hand (pivoting from shoulder)
arc described by hand (pivoting from elbow)

Hands should move in opposite directions in a symmetrical motion.

Arrange the materials and tools in the order in which they are used.

Improvement Example

Reducing the walking distance

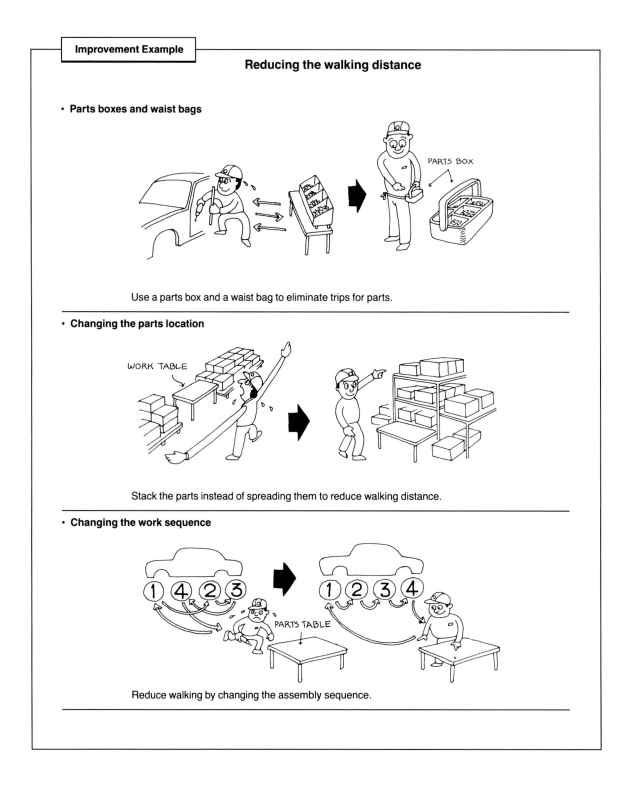

- **Parts boxes and waist bags**

PARTS BOX

Use a parts box and a waist bag to eliminate trips for parts.

- **Changing the parts location**

WORK TABLE

Stack the parts instead of spreading them to reduce walking distance.

- **Changing the work sequence**

PARTS TABLE

Reduce walking by changing the assembly sequence.

| Improvement Example |

Minimizing the walking distance for an oiling operation

• **Problem identification:**

A worker makes a trip several times a day from the oil storage room to different machines for inspection and oiling. It is believed that the worker is walking more than necessary.

• **Current condition:**

Average number of round trips between oil storage room and machines: 8 trips per day
Walking time: 2.5 hours per day (8 hours)

• **Causes for unnecessary walking:**

1. Forgetting the tools needed for oiling.
2. Running low on oil.
3. No order established for inspecting and oiling the machines.
4. Best route for inspecting and oiling is not established.

• **Improvements:**

1. A handcart was fabricated for carrying the tools and oil to the machines.
2. The shortest route for oiling the machines was determined by actually timing the different routes.

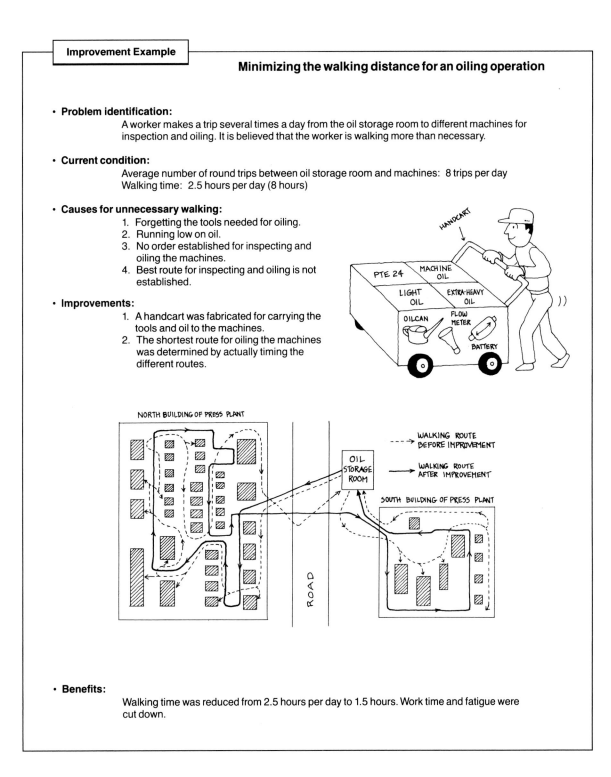

• **Benefits:**

Walking time was reduced from 2.5 hours per day to 1.5 hours. Work time and fatigue were cut down.

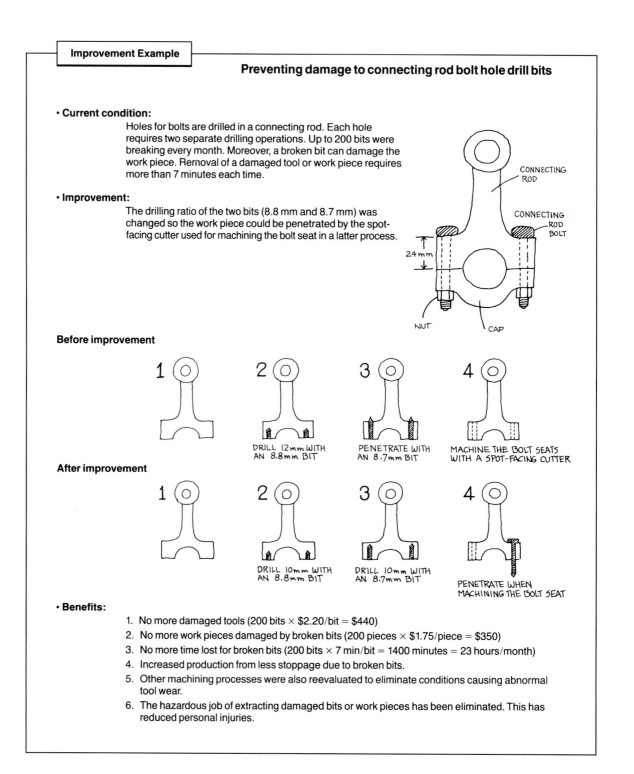

Improvement Example

Preventing damage to connecting rod bolt hole drill bits

• Current condition:

Holes for bolts are drilled in a connecting rod. Each hole requires two separate drilling operations. Up to 200 bits were breaking every month. Moreover, a broken bit can damage the work piece. Removal of a damaged tool or work piece requires more than 7 minutes each time.

• Improvement:

The drilling ratio of the two bits (8.8 mm and 8.7 mm) was changed so the work piece could be penetrated by the spot-facing cutter used for machining the bolt seat in a latter process.

CONNECTING ROD

CONNECTING ROD BOLT

24 mm

NUT   CAP

Before improvement

1

2 DRILL 12mm WITH AN 8.8mm BIT

3 PENETRATE WITH AN 8.7mm BIT

4 MACHINE THE BOLT SEATS WITH A SPOT-FACING CUTTER

After improvement

1

2 DRILL 10mm WITH AN 8.8mm BIT

3 DRILL 10mm WITH AN 8.7mm BIT

4 PENETRATE WHEN MACHINING THE BOLT SEAT

• Benefits:

1. No more damaged tools (200 bits × \$2.20/bit = \$440)
2. No more work pieces damaged by broken bits (200 pieces × \$1.75/piece = \$350)
3. No more time lost for broken bits (200 bits × 7 min/bit = 1400 minutes = 23 hours/month)
4. Increased production from less stoppage due to broken bits.
5. Other machining processes were also reevaluated to eliminate conditions causing abnormal tool wear.
6. The hazardous job of extracting damaged bits or work pieces has been eliminated. This has reduced personal injuries.

Improvements in Tools, Machinery, and Equipment

Identifying Potential Improvements

The natural order in workplace improvement is to start with the reduction of wasted motion and then move on to the improvement of tools, machinery, and equipment. For operators, this progression means first solving what is familiar. For management, it means first making less costly changes. You can experiment a bit with a worker's motions, but it's difficult to undo an equipment or machinery modification. However, even though equipment and machinery modification is difficult, it can pay off well if done properly.

Identifying candidates for improvements in tools

- Mechanize manual tasks.
- Use a holding tool to hold something for a long time.
- Move in the same direction that the equipment moves.
- Combine two or more tools into one.
- Use a mechanism that allows tightening of the tool with minimal movement.
- Use tools and equipment that allow materials and parts to be grabbed easily.
- Use tools that allow both hands to work at the same time.
- Use tools and guides to restrict the path of movement.
- Design tools to allow positional alignment from a comfortable viewing position.
- Design tools and machines to make a resounding "click" when they are ready for operation.
- Use gravity.
- Use magnets.
- Reduce the weight.
- Use a motor.
- Use air pressure.
- Let it vibrate.

Identifying candidates for improvements in machinery and on the workbench

- Use a simple attachment.
- Change the height of the workbench.
- Change the distance between machines.

- Put two machines next to each other.
- Eliminate transportation between processes.
- Make the people move.
- Make the material move.
- Reverse the position of the machines.

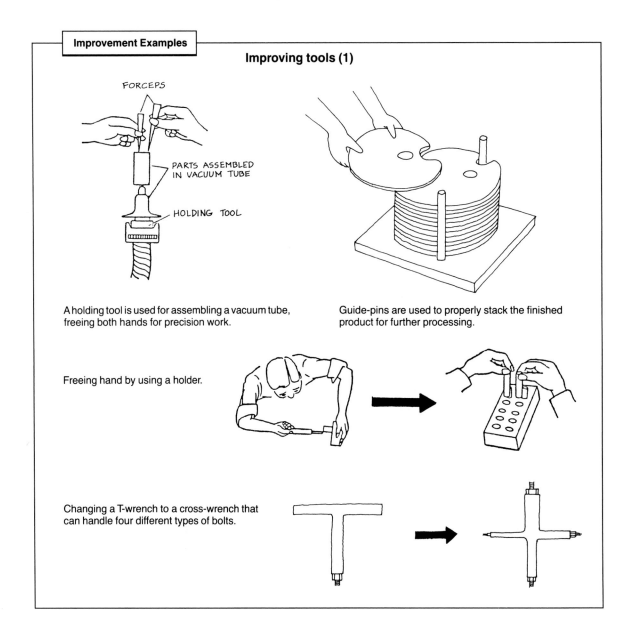

Improvement Examples

Improving tools (1)

A holding tool is used for assembling a vacuum tube, freeing both hands for precision work.

Guide-pins are used to properly stack the finished product for further processing.

Freeing hand by using a holder.

Changing a T-wrench to a cross-wrench that can handle four different types of bolts.

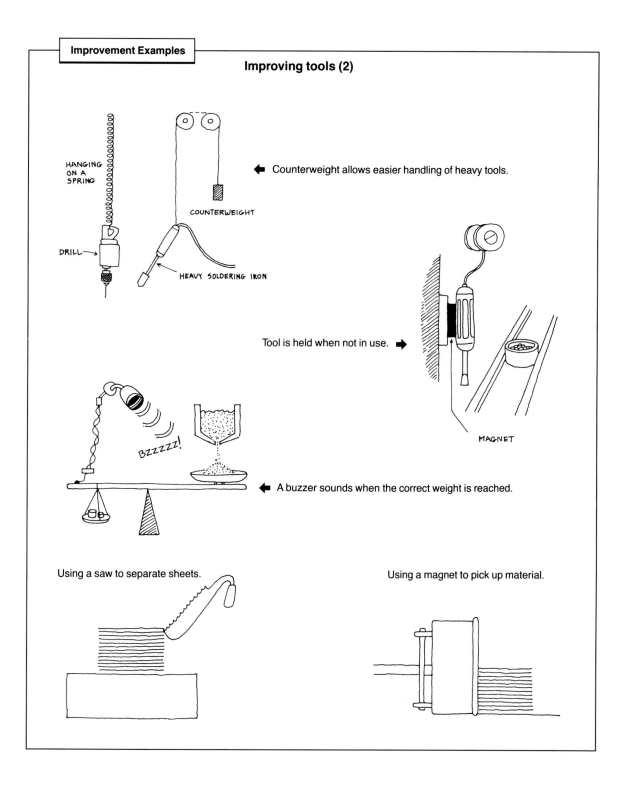

Improvement Examples

Improving tools (2)

HANGING ON A SPRING

DRILL →

Counterweight allows easier handling of heavy tools.

COUNTERWEIGHT

HEAVY SOLDERING IRON

Tool is held when not in use. →

MAGNET

BZZZZZ!

A buzzer sounds when the correct weight is reached.

Using a saw to separate sheets.

Using a magnet to pick up material.

Improvement Examples

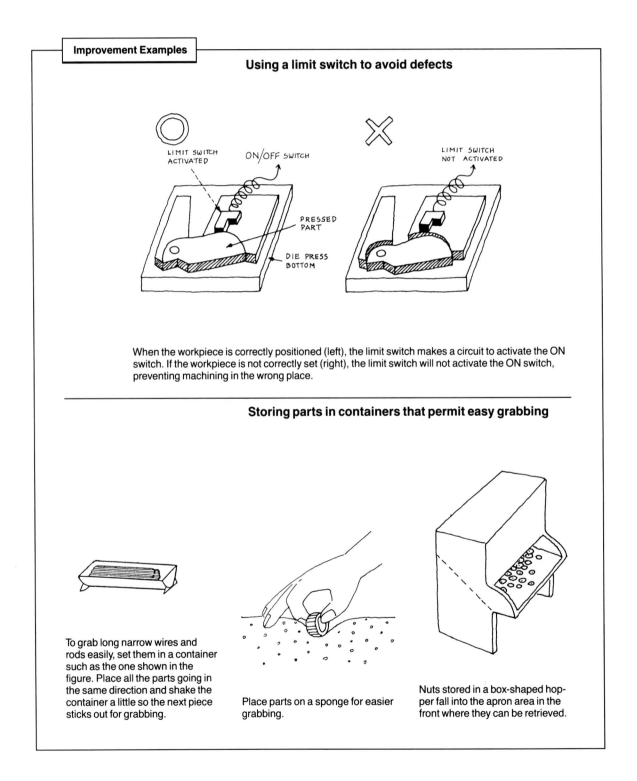

Using a limit switch to avoid defects

When the workpiece is correctly positioned (left), the limit switch makes a circuit to activate the ON switch. If the workpiece is not correctly set (right), the limit switch will not activate the ON switch, preventing machining in the wrong place.

Storing parts in containers that permit easy grabbing

To grab long narrow wires and rods easily, set them in a container such as the one shown in the figure. Place all the parts going in the same direction and shake the container a little so the next piece sticks out for grabbing.

Place parts on a sponge for easier grabbing.

Nuts stored in a box-shaped hopper fall into the apron area in the front where they can be retrieved.

Improvement Example

Pliers with a device to hold the workpiece after cutting

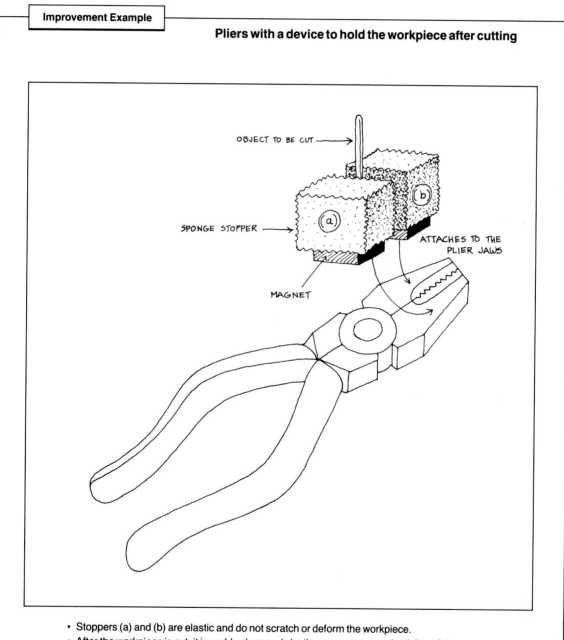

OBJECT TO BE CUT

SPONGE STOPPER

MAGNET

ATTACHES TO THE PLIER JAWS

- Stoppers (a) and (b) are elastic and do not scratch or deform the workpiece.
- After the workpiece is cut, it is grabbed securely by the sponge, preventing it from flying away.
- The sponge stoppers are easily attached and detached.

(proposed by Beaker Circle, Kure Plant, Nisshin Steel; utility model registration pending)

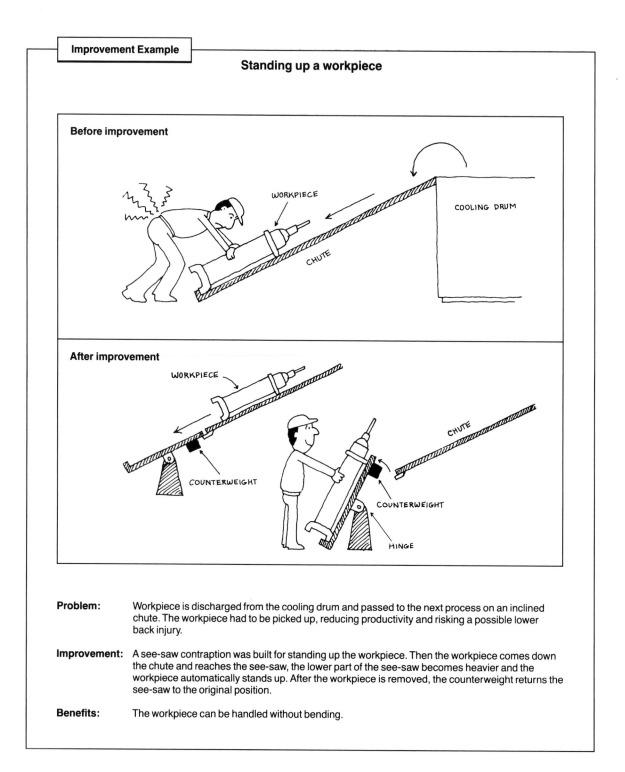

Improvement Example

Standing up a workpiece

Before improvement

WORKPIECE

COOLING DRUM

CHUTE

After improvement

WORKPIECE

COUNTERWEIGHT

CHUTE

COUNTERWEIGHT

HINGE

Problem: Workpiece is discharged from the cooling drum and passed to the next process on an inclined chute. The workpiece had to be picked up, reducing productivity and risking a possible lower back injury.

Improvement: A see-saw contraption was built for standing up the workpiece. Then the workpiece comes down the chute and reaches the see-saw, the lower part of the see-saw becomes heavier and the workpiece automatically stands up. After the workpiece is removed, the counterweight returns the see-saw to the original position.

Benefits: The workpiece can be handled without bending.

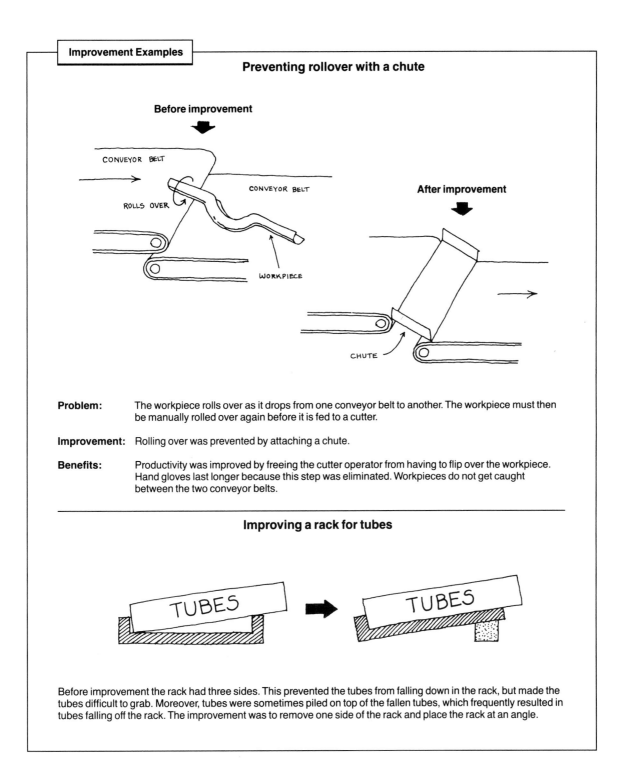

Improvement Examples

Preventing rollover with a chute

Before improvement

CONVEYOR BELT

CONVEYOR BELT

ROLLS OVER

WORKPIECE

After improvement

CHUTE

Problem: The workpiece rolls over as it drops from one conveyor belt to another. The workpiece must then be manually rolled over again before it is fed to a cutter.

Improvement: Rolling over was prevented by attaching a chute.

Benefits: Productivity was improved by freeing the cutter operator from having to flip over the workpiece. Hand gloves last longer because this step was eliminated. Workpieces do not get caught between the two conveyor belts.

Improving a rack for tubes

TUBES   TUBES

Before improvement the rack had three sides. This prevented the tubes from falling down in the rack, but made the tubes difficult to grab. Moreover, tubes were sometimes piled on top of the fallen tubes, which frequently resulted in tubes falling off the rack. The improvement was to remove one side of the rack and place the rack at an angle.

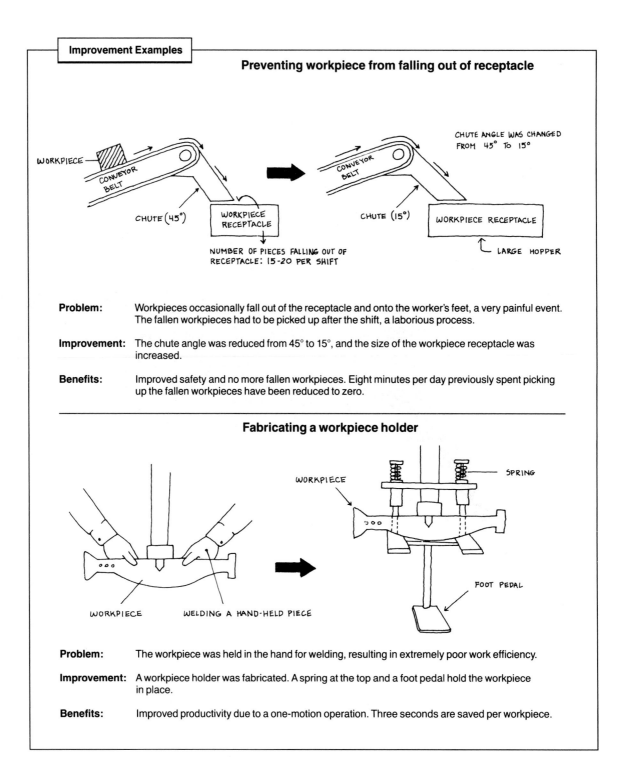

Improvement Examples

Preventing workpiece from falling out of receptacle

Problem: Workpieces occasionally fall out of the receptacle and onto the worker's feet, a very painful event. The fallen workpieces had to be picked up after the shift, a laborious process.

Improvement: The chute angle was reduced from 45° to 15°, and the size of the workpiece receptacle was increased.

Benefits: Improved safety and no more fallen workpieces. Eight minutes per day previously spent picking up the fallen workpieces have been reduced to zero.

Fabricating a workpiece holder

Problem: The workpiece was held in the hand for welding, resulting in extremely poor work efficiency.

Improvement: A workpiece holder was fabricated. A spring at the top and a foot pedal hold the workpiece in place.

Benefits: Improved productivity due to a one-motion operation. Three seconds are saved per workpiece.

Improvement Example

One-motion replacement of hex nut wrench attachment and screwdriver bit

Current condition:

Footrest for an automobile was being attached in the following way:

1. Tighten bolt.
2. Replace hex nut attachment with screwdriver bit.
3. Tighten screw.

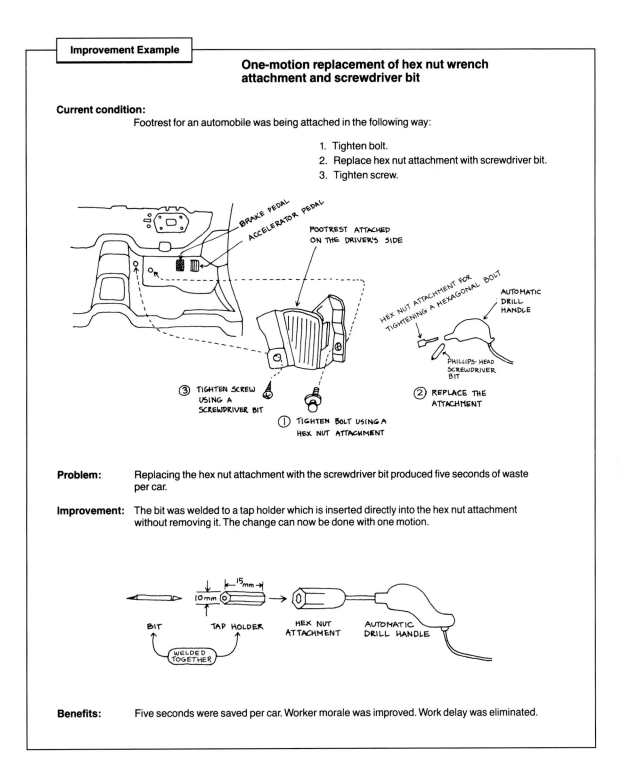

Problem: Replacing the hex nut attachment with the screwdriver bit produced five seconds of waste per car.

Improvement: The bit was welded to a tap holder which is inserted directly into the hex nut attachment without removing it. The change can now be done with one motion.

Benefits: Five seconds were saved per car. Worker morale was improved. Work delay was eliminated.

Improvement Example

Device for attaching a pipe opening to tank

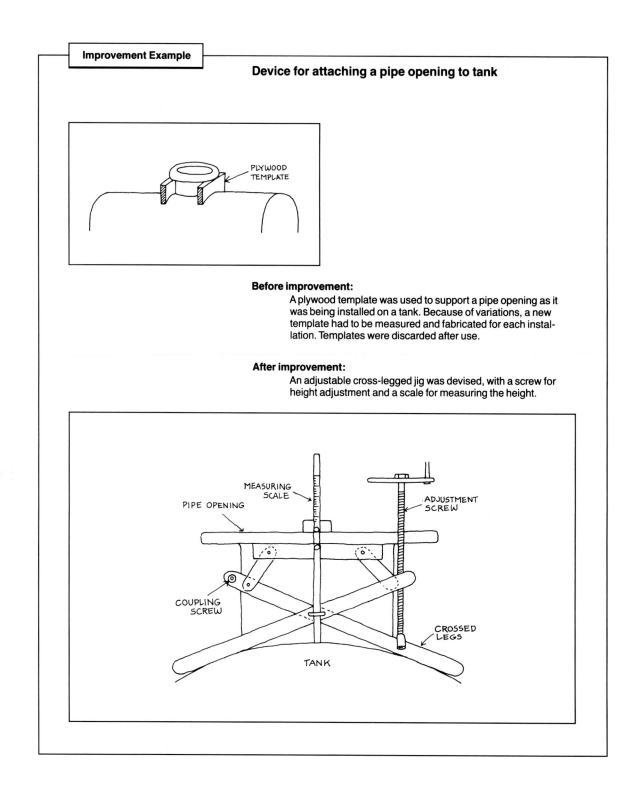

Before improvement:

A plywood template was used to support a pipe opening as it was being installed on a tank. Because of variations, a new template had to be measured and fabricated for each installation. Templates were discarded after use.

After improvement:

An adjustable cross-legged jig was devised, with a screw for height adjustment and a scale for measuring the height.

Improvement Example

Mistake-proof way of preventing unfinished work from being passed downstream

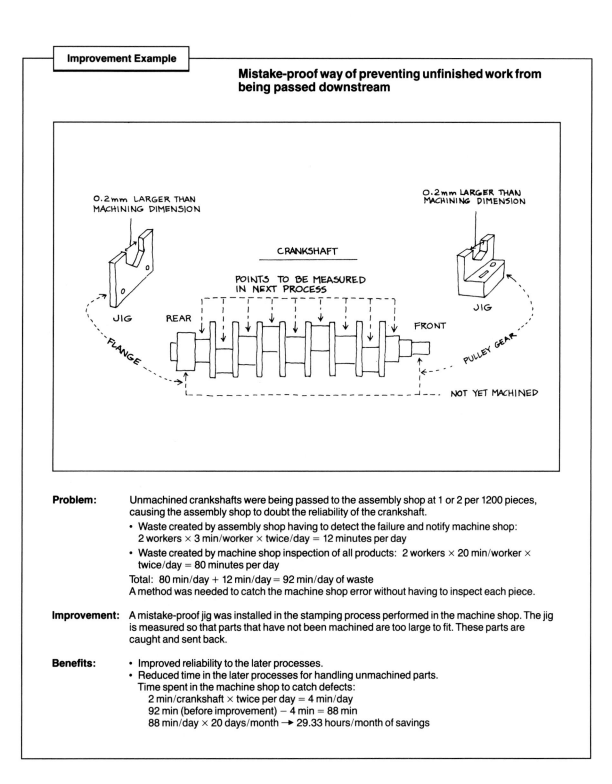

Problem: Unmachined crankshafts were being passed to the assembly shop at 1 or 2 per 1200 pieces, causing the assembly shop to doubt the reliability of the crankshaft.

- Waste created by assembly shop having to detect the failure and notify machine shop: 2 workers × 3 min/worker × twice/day = 12 minutes per day
- Waste created by machine shop inspection of all products: 2 workers × 20 min/worker × twice/day = 80 minutes per day

Total: 80 min/day + 12 min/day = 92 min/day of waste
A method was needed to catch the machine shop error without having to inspect each piece.

Improvement: A mistake-proof jig was installed in the stamping process performed in the machine shop. The jig is measured so that parts that have not been machined are too large to fit. These parts are caught and sent back.

Benefits:
- Improved reliability to the later processes.
- Reduced time in the later processes for handling unmachined parts.
  Time spent in the machine shop to catch defects:
  2 min/crankshaft × twice per day = 4 min/day
  92 min (before improvement) − 4 min = 88 min
  88 min/day × 20 days/month → 29.33 hours/month of savings

Improvement Example

Device for loading aluminum ore

Problem: Aluminum ore had to be manually loaded into a melting
furnace, a very laborious task.

Improvement: A hoist is used to dump the ore in front of an inserter. The
inserter, which is pushed by a jig attached to a forklift,
pushes the ore into the melting furnace.

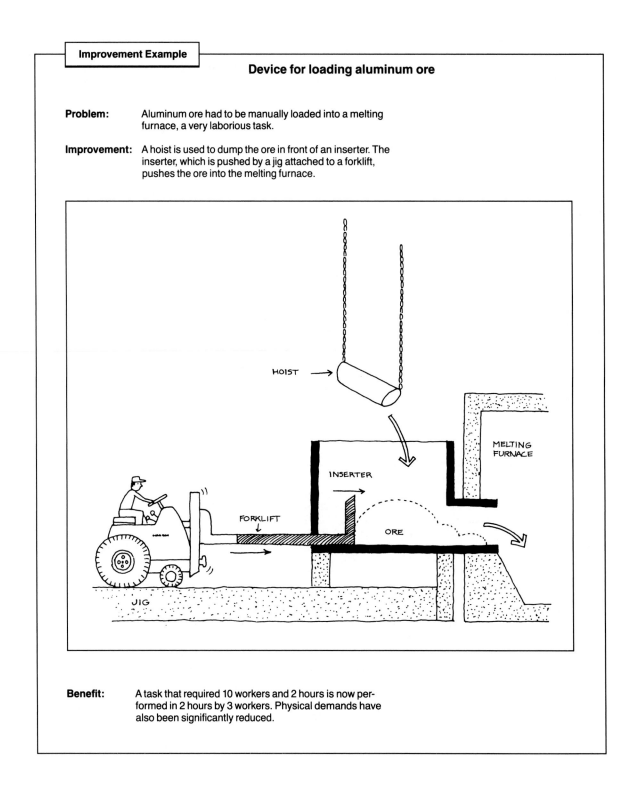

Benefit: A task that required 10 workers and 2 hours is now performed in 2 hours by 3 workers. Physical demands have
also been significantly reduced.

Improvement Example

Improved dimensional accuracy of core print for L-type head port

Current condition:

A port core is used to cast exhaust ports in an L-type cylinder head. The current molding-firing time for producing the part cores must be reduced from 1 minute 20 seconds to 30 seconds for mass production.

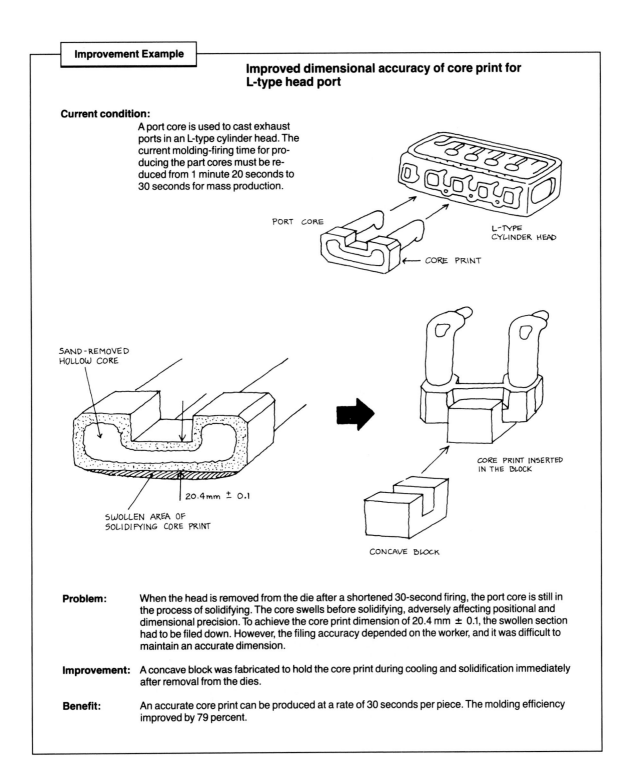

PORT CORE

L-TYPE CYLINDER HEAD

CORE PRINT

SAND-REMOVED HOLLOW CORE

20.4mm ± 0.1

SWOLLEN AREA OF SOLIDIFYING CORE PRINT

CORE PRINT INSERTED IN THE BLOCK

CONCAVE BLOCK

Problem: When the head is removed from the die after a shortened 30-second firing, the port core is still in the process of solidifying. The core swells before solidifying, adversely affecting positional and dimensional precision. To achieve the core print dimension of 20.4 mm ± 0.1, the swollen section had to be filed down. However, the filing accuracy depended on the worker, and it was difficult to maintain an accurate dimension.

Improvement: A concave block was fabricated to hold the core print during cooling and solidification immediately after removal from the dies.

Benefit: An accurate core print can be produced at a rate of 30 seconds per piece. The molding efficiency improved by 79 percent.

Improvement Example

Improved method for cooling the welder electrode

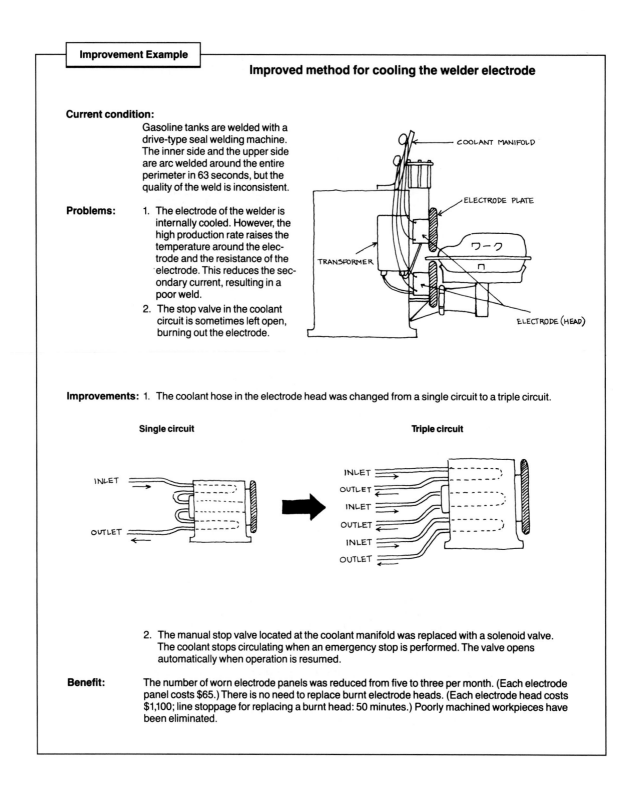

Current condition:
Gasoline tanks are welded with a drive-type seal welding machine. The inner side and the upper side are arc welded around the entire perimeter in 63 seconds, but the quality of the weld is inconsistent.

Problems:
1. The electrode of the welder is internally cooled. However, the high production rate raises the temperature around the electrode and the resistance of the electrode. This reduces the secondary current, resulting in a poor weld.
2. The stop valve in the coolant circuit is sometimes left open, burning out the electrode.

COOLANT MANIFOLD

ELECTRODE PLATE

TRANSFORMER

ELECTRODE (HEAD)

Improvements: 1. The coolant hose in the electrode head was changed from a single circuit to a triple circuit.

Single circuit

INLET

OUTLET

Triple circuit

INLET
OUTLET
INLET
OUTLET
INLET
OUTLET

2. The manual stop valve located at the coolant manifold was replaced with a solenoid valve. The coolant stops circulating when an emergency stop is performed. The valve opens automatically when operation is resumed.

Benefit:
The number of worn electrode panels was reduced from five to three per month. (Each electrode panel costs $65.) There is no need to replace burnt electrode heads. (Each electrode head costs $1,100; line stoppage for replacing a burnt head: 50 minutes.) Poorly machined workpieces have been eliminated.

Improvement Example

Installation of a failure alarm panel

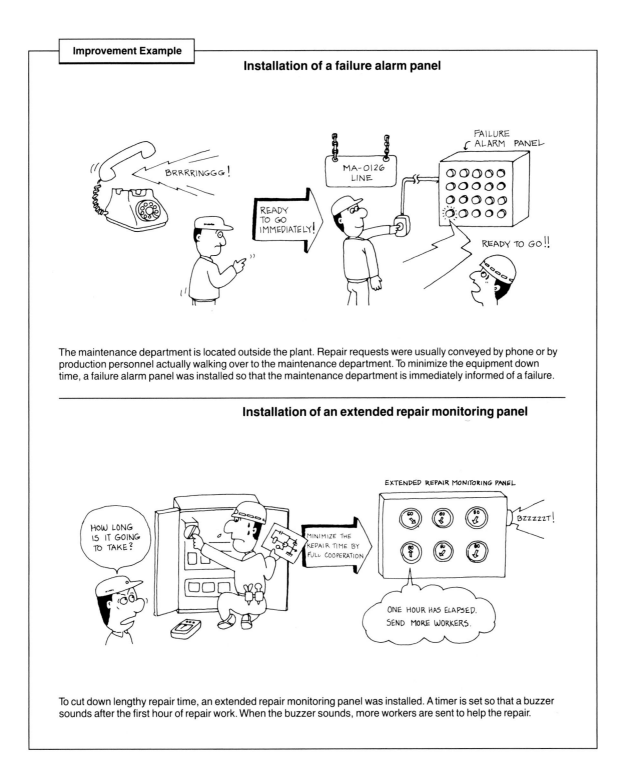

The maintenance department is located outside the plant. Repair requests were usually conveyed by phone or by production personnel actually walking over to the maintenance department. To minimize the equipment down time, a failure alarm panel was installed so that the maintenance department is immediately informed of a failure.

Installation of an extended repair monitoring panel

To cut down lengthy repair time, an extended repair monitoring panel was installed. A timer is set so that a buzzer sounds after the first hour of repair work. When the buzzer sounds, more workers are sent to help the repair.

Improvement Example

Kanban system for electrical parts

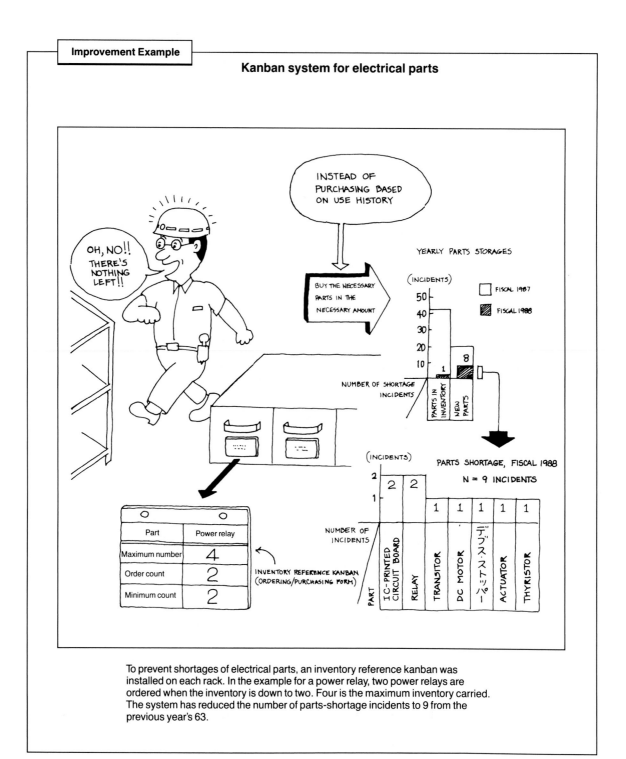

To prevent shortages of electrical parts, an inventory reference kanban was installed on each rack. In the example for a power relay, two power relays are ordered when the inventory is down to two. Four is the maximum inventory carried. The system has reduced the number of parts-shortage incidents to 9 from the previous year's 63.

Improvements in Organization and Safety
Identifying Potential Improvements

Eliminating unsafe conditions in the workplace is central to an improvement suggestion activity. It is impossible for management to know all safety-related problems. Safety must be pursued by all workers: each person must consider ways to improve hazardous conditions. Safety awareness is improved by worker programs that emphasize safe practices and set-ups.

Things to look for in improving organization and orderliness

- Can like objects be kept together?
- Is too much time being spent for searching?
- Can color-coding be used?
- Can it be discarded?
- Are frequently used things stored near where they are used?
- Are seldom used things stored farther away?
- Can something be eliminated?
- Can a partition be set up?

Identifying candidates for safety improvement

- Is a rotating part exposed?
- Is a safety valve rusted together?
- Is an electrical cord worn out?
- Is the floor too slippery?
- Should a handrail be installed?
- Are heavy objects being moved manually?
- Are workers too familiar with an operation?
- Is it necessary to touch the part?
- Can sound be used?
- Can visual displays be used?
- Can a mirror be used?
- Should a time period be established?

Mistake-proofing the workplace

- Make the object identifiable by shape, size, color, feel, sound, and so on.

- Use jigs and tools to prevent mistakes.
- Sort objects by the way they are stored, the order in which they are used, and so on.
- Devise automatic checks so that tasks cannot mistakenly be performed out of sequence.

Improvement Example

Cable protection device

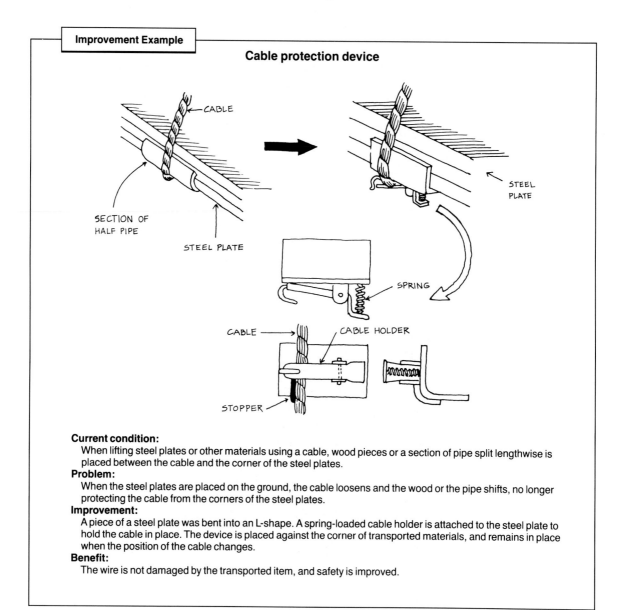

Current condition:
When lifting steel plates or other materials using a cable, wood pieces or a section of pipe split lengthwise is placed between the cable and the corner of the steel plates.

Problem:
When the steel plates are placed on the ground, the cable loosens and the wood or the pipe shifts, no longer protecting the cable from the corners of the steel plates.

Improvement:
A piece of a steel plate was bent into an L-shape. A spring-loaded cable holder is attached to the steel plate to hold the cable in place. The device is placed against the corner of transported materials, and remains in place when the position of the cable changes.

Benefit:
The wire is not damaged by the transported item, and safety is improved.

Improvement Example

Mistake-proofing

People make mistakes regardless of how intelligent or careful they are. Measures should be provided to prevent mistakes. This is "mistake-proofing."

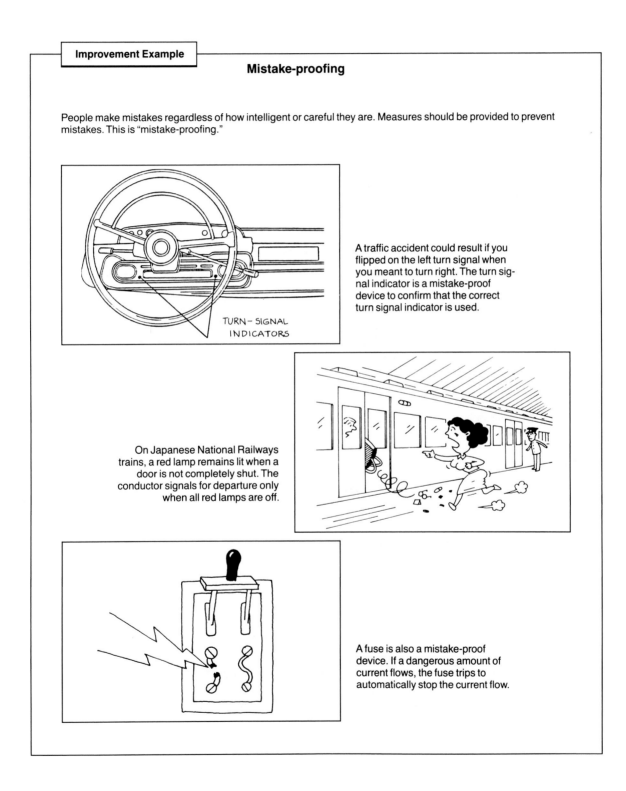

A traffic accident could result if you flipped on the left turn signal when you meant to turn right. The turn signal indicator is a mistake-proof device to confirm that the correct turn signal indicator is used.

TURN-SIGNAL INDICATORS

On Japanese National Railways trains, a red lamp remains lit when a door is not completely shut. The conductor signals for departure only when all red lamps are off.

A fuse is also a mistake-proof device. If a dangerous amount of current flows, the fuse trips to automatically stop the current flow.

Improvement Example	Improved tool-setting device

Before improvement

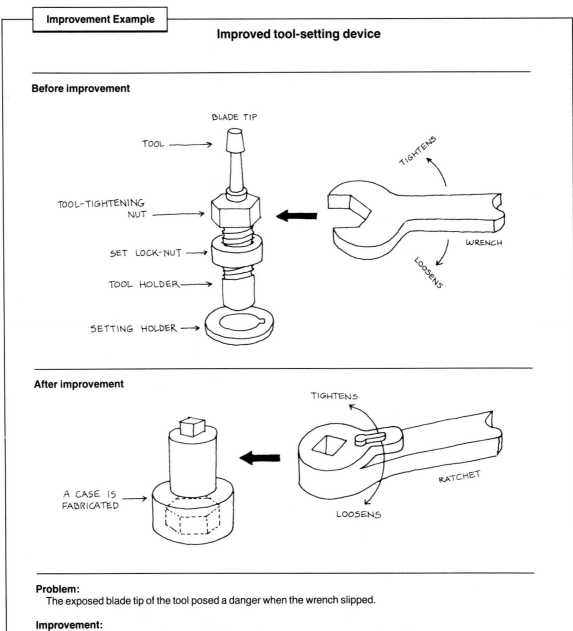

Problem:
The exposed blade tip of the tool posed a danger when the wrench slipped.

Improvement:
The tool, including the blade tip, is covered with a case. A ratchet is used instead of an open wrench.

Benefit:
The danger of injury from a slipped wrench is eliminated. There is no need to reposition the wrench. This improves safety and productivity.

Improvements in Transportation

Identifying Potential Improvements

Transporting includes not only the moving of goods but also all activities incidental to it, such as stacking and unstacking. Since transportation costs account for 25 to 40 percent of the processing cost of a good, eliminating wasteful transportation is an effective way to cut costs.

Basic rules of transportation

- Design the layout and work sequence to minimize transportation distance.
- Combine tasks to reduce the number of trips.
- Make the load neither too heavy nor too light. Use the return trip for transport as well.
- Increase the moving speed during transport.
- Use machines as much as possible; eliminate manual transportation.
- Compare and determine whether it is better to move the goods or to move the workers.
- Transportation should be performed by specialists; do not have workers transport the goods.

Basic rules of storage

- Store similar items together.
- Sort items as you store them.
- Use space three-dimensionally.
- Store heavy objects on the bottom, light objects on top.
- Store so that the quantity remaining is obvious.
- Use older items first.
- Store frequently used items at the front and infrequently used items farther back.
- Provide pallets and boxes to eliminate repacking.

Identifying potential improvements

- Can the transportation be made more convenient?
- Can the transporting be eliminated?
- Can the transportation distance be reduced?

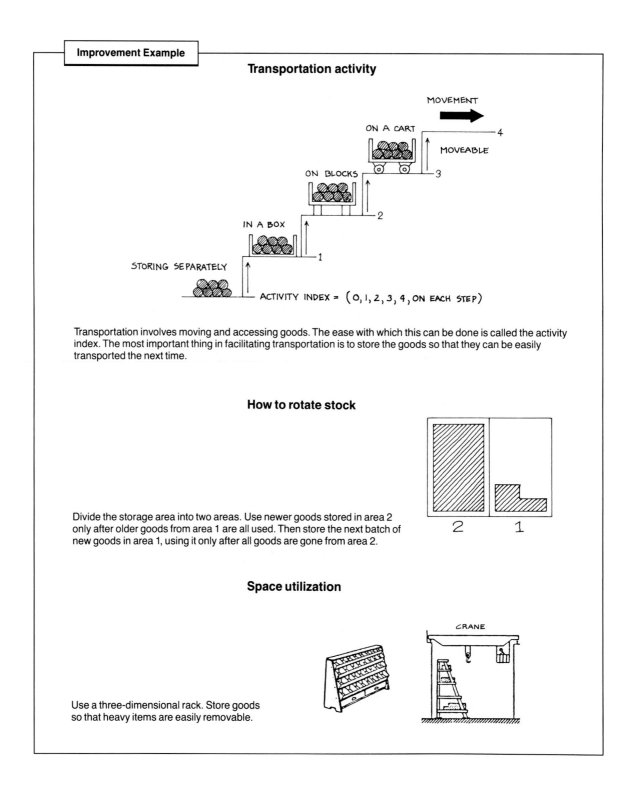

Improvement Example

Transportation activity

Transportation involves moving and accessing goods. The ease with which this can be done is called the activity index. The most important thing in facilitating transportation is to store the goods so that they can be easily transported the next time.

How to rotate stock

Divide the storage area into two areas. Use newer goods stored in area 2 only after older goods from area 1 are all used. Then store the next batch of new goods in area 1, using it only after all goods are gone from area 2.

Space utilization

Use a three-dimensional rack. Store goods so that heavy items are easily removable.

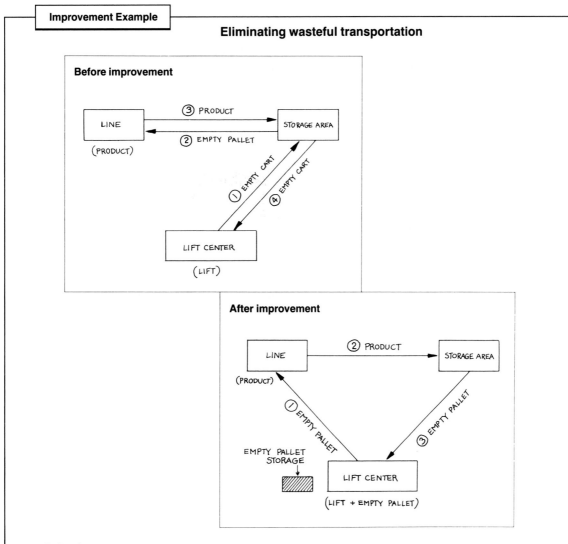

Improvement Example

Eliminating wasteful transportation

Before improvement

After improvement

Before improvement:
When the lift center receives a request from the line to transport a product, a forklift goes to a storage area to retrieve an empty pallet. The pallet is taken to the line and loaded with the product, which is then taken to the storage area. An empty forklift then returns to the lift center.

After improvement:
A storage area for empty pallets was constructed near the lift center, eliminating an empty trip to the storage area. After the product is delivered to the storage area, the forklift returns the empty pallet to its storage area for next use.

Benefits:
Unnecessary transportation has been eliminated, improving the transportation efficiency.

Improvement Example

Reducing the amount of floc produced in processing water-soluble cutting-fluid waste

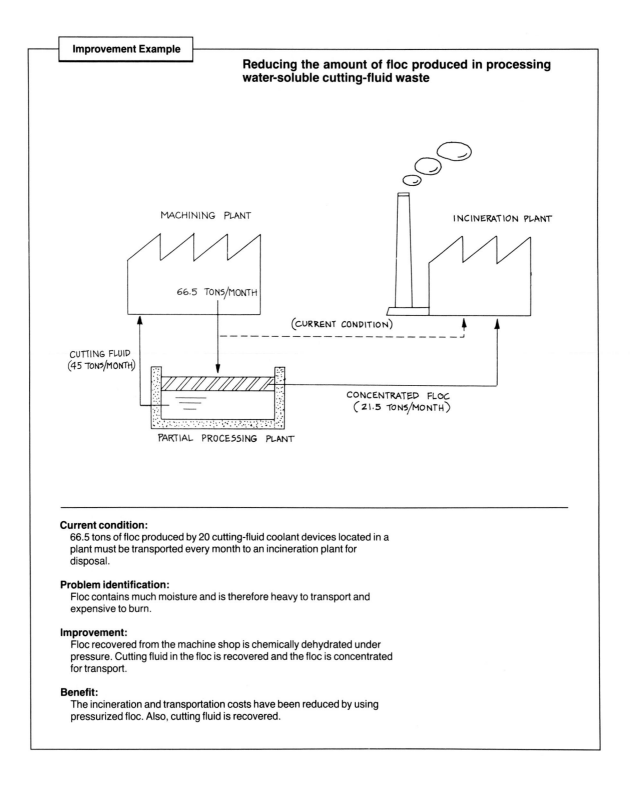

Current condition:
66.5 tons of floc produced by 20 cutting-fluid coolant devices located in a plant must be transported every month to an incineration plant for disposal.

Problem identification:
Floc contains much moisture and is therefore heavy to transport and expensive to burn.

Improvement:
Floc recovered from the machine shop is chemically dehydrated under pressure. Cutting fluid in the floc is recovered and the floc is concentrated for transport.

Benefit:
The incineration and transportation costs have been reduced by using pressurized floc. Also, cutting fluid is recovered.

Improvement Example

Fabrication of grease-carrier cart

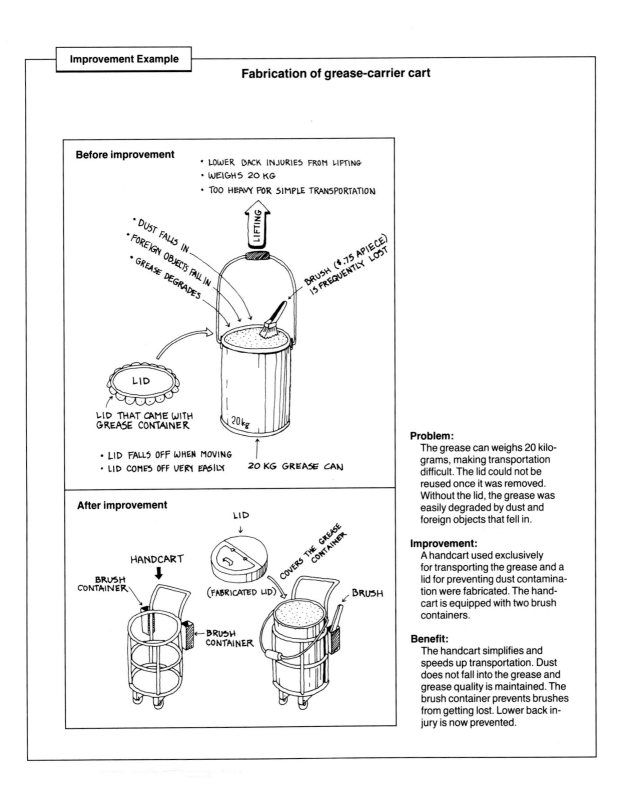

Before improvement

- LOWER BACK INJURIES FROM LIFTING
- WEIGHS 20 KG
- TOO HEAVY FOR SIMPLE TRANSPORTATION

LIFTING

- DUST FALLS IN
- FOREIGN OBJECTS FALL IN
- GREASE DEGRADES

BRUSH ($.75 APIECE) IS FREQUENTLY LOST

LID

LID THAT CAME WITH GREASE CONTAINER

- LID FALLS OFF WHEN MOVING
- LID COMES OFF VERY EASILY

20 KG GREASE CAN

20 kg

After improvement

LID

HANDCART

COVERS THE GREASE CONTAINER

BRUSH CONTAINER

(FABRICATED LID)

BRUSH

BRUSH CONTAINER

Problem:
The grease can weighs 20 kilograms, making transportation difficult. The lid could not be reused once it was removed. Without the lid, the grease was easily degraded by dust and foreign objects that fell in.

Improvement:
A handcart used exclusively for transporting the grease and a lid for preventing dust contamination were fabricated. The handcart is equipped with two brush containers.

Benefit:
The handcart simplifies and speeds up transportation. Dust does not fall into the grease and grease quality is maintained. The brush container prevents brushes from getting lost. Lower back injury is now prevented.

Improvement Example

Collapsible scaffold

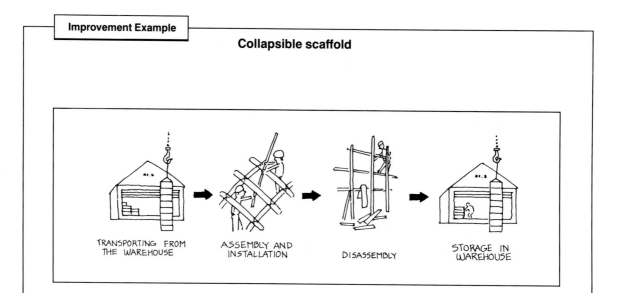

TRANSPORTING FROM THE WAREHOUSE → ASSEMBLY AND INSTALLATION → DISASSEMBLY → STORAGE IN WAREHOUSE

Problem:
Scaffolding used for shipbuilding must be assembled and disassembled after each use, involving a considerable amount of labor and cost for transportation from the warehouse, assembly, and so on.

Problem identification:
To simplify the assembly and installation. One solution is to store the assembled scaffold, which would waste considerable space. What other ways could it be simplified?

Improvement:
The scaffold was divided into collapsible sections, which makes it easier to store in a warehouse.

Benefit:
Three-quarters of the labor and time required for assembly and installation of a scaffold was eliminated. Assembly space is no longer needed.

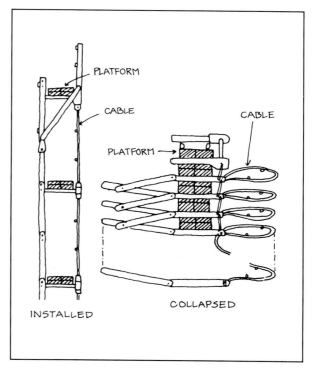

PLATFORM
CABLE
PLATFORM
CABLE
INSTALLED
COLLAPSED

Improvements in Cost-Cutting
Identifying Potential Improvements

Cost reduction concepts — materials

- Pay less for the materials.
- Substitute effective but less expensive materials.
- Use extra or unused materials.
- Reduce the number of defective components from subcontractors.
- Redesign the parts to cost less.
- Reduce the inventory of materials.
- Prevent degradation of materials and parts during storage.

Cost reduction concepts — processing

- Reduce equipment down time.
- Use new equipment.
- Increase the operating speed of the equipment.
- Change the design to simplify processing.
- Improve the flow of goods or the plant layout.

Cost reduction concepts — labor

- Mechanize manual tasks.
- Reduce the number of inspection personnel, or automate the inspection process.
- Increase the number of tasks handled by one worker.
- Mechanize manual transportation or use conveyor belts.
- Balance the work load among employees working as a team.
- Automate, or reduce the amount of labor required in an operation.

Cost reduction concepts — overhead expenses

- Reduce repair costs through preventive maintenance; increase efficiency.
- Reduce inventory.
- Simplify clerical tasks.
- Shorten the delivery deadline; reduce the amount of work-in-process.

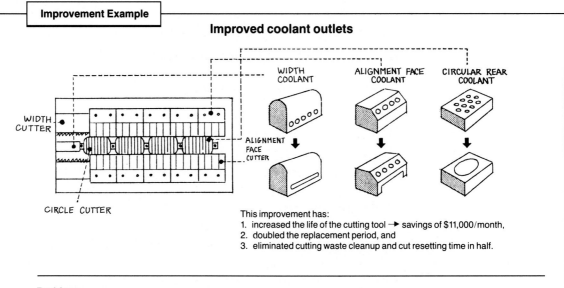

Improvement Example

Improved coolant outlets

This improvement has:
1. increased the life of the cutting tool → savings of $11,000/month,
2. doubled the replacement period, and
3. eliminated cutting waste cleanup and cut resetting time in half.

Problem:
The blade of a tool used to cut steel parts had to be replaced every 3,000-4,000 pieces, requiring disassembly of the machine. The blade wore out because threads from gloves worn while cleaning the cutting scrap block the outlets for the coolant that protects the cutting blade. Removing the threads itself requires much time.

Improvement:
Over seven months of experimentation, used blades were examined, the size of the coolant holes was changed many times, and the oil pressure was increased. As a result, the coolant oil hole was increased in size as shown above.

Benefits:
Threads no longer clog the oil outlet holes. The tool maintenance time has been cut in half. Improved oil supply has reduced the wear on blades, increasing their life by two to three times. The savings in blade-related costs are $11,000 per month.

- Increase the lifespan of secondary materials used in processing.
- Promote better organization and orderliness to eliminate excessive storage.

Identifying potential improvements through value analysis

- Is this item irreplaceable?
- Can standard or commercially available items be used?
- Is there a higher quality item available?
- What value does this item possess?
- Is the cost of the item justified by its performance?
- Is there a less expensive production method?

- Can waste be eliminated by changing the shape?
- Can the tolerance for variation be increased?
- Can alternatives or substitutes be used?
- Can a different material be used?
- Are the material costs, indirect costs, and profit reasonable?
- Is there a way to reduce the costs of materials?

Improvement Example

Increasing the cutting area of a disposable blade

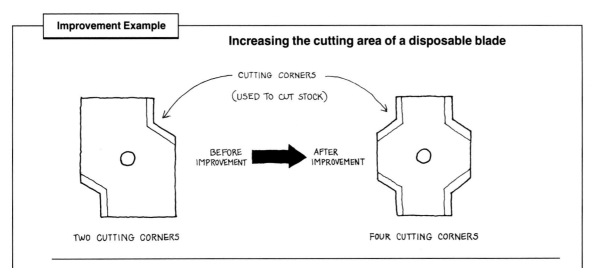

Current condition:
Only two corners of a tool used for cutting the outer diameter of a crankshaft can be used. The tool is installed on a holder and its dimensions are not adjustable. Moreover, it cannot be reground and must be discarded after use. Each piece costs $7.40 and an average of 75 pieces are used every month.

Problem identification:
1. Can the life of the tool be increased?
2. Can the tool be reground?
3. Can the number of cutting corners be increased?

Improvements:
1. Increasing the life of the tool is impossible due to the cutting conditions.
2. Regrinding the tool is impossible with the particular machine.
3. To increase the number of cutting corners, the blade was changed as shown. The tool holder was changed so that a four-corner tool could be installed.

Benefit:
The unit cost increased by $.46 but the cost of using the tool decreased with the increased number of cutting corners.

Before improvement: $7.40/tool × 75 tools/ month = $556
After improvement: $7.86/tool × 38 tools/month = $298
$258 saved per month.

How to Increase Value (V)

$$V \text{ (value)} = \frac{F \text{ (function)}}{C \text{ (cost)}}$$

	1	2	3	4
Function (F)	↑	↑	↑	→
Cost (C)	↓	→	↑	↓

To increase value (V):

1. Increase functionality while reducing cost.
2. Increase functionality while keeping the same cost.
3. Increase functionality more than the increase in cost.
4. Keep the same functionality while reducing cost. Traditional value analysis stressed the fourth method — reducing cost. In the future, attention should be focused on using the first three methods to increase the functionality.

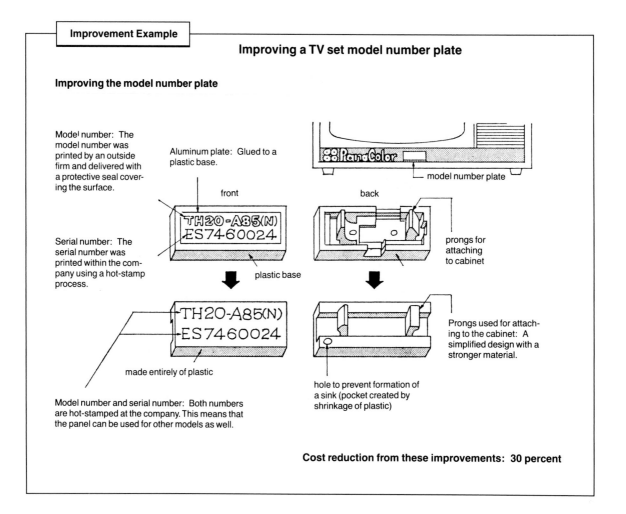

Improvement Example

Improving a TV set model number plate

Improving the model number plate

Model number: The model number was printed by an outside firm and delivered with a protective seal covering the surface.

Aluminum plate: Glued to a plastic base.

model number plate

front

back

TH20-A85(N)
ES7460024

prongs for attaching to cabinet

Serial number: The serial number was printed within the company using a hot-stamp process.

plastic base

TH20-A85(N)
ES7460024

Prongs used for attaching to the cabinet: A simplified design with a stronger material.

made entirely of plastic

hole to prevent formation of a sink (pocket created by shrinkage of plastic)

Model number and serial number: Both numbers are hot-stamped at the company. This means that the panel can be used for other models as well.

Cost reduction from these improvements: 30 percent

Improvement Examples

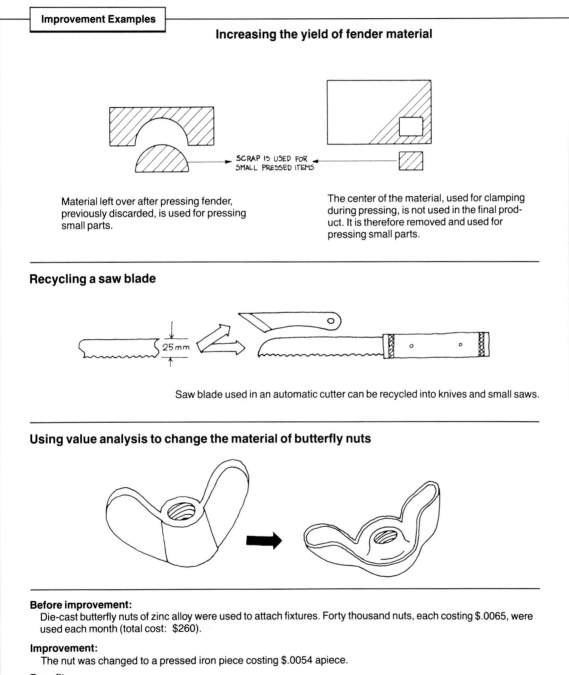

Increasing the yield of fender material

SCRAP IS USED FOR SMALL PRESSED ITEMS

Material left over after pressing fender, previously discarded, is used for pressing small parts.

The center of the material, used for clamping during pressing, is not used in the final product. It is therefore removed and used for pressing small parts.

Recycling a saw blade

25 mm

Saw blade used in an automatic cutter can be recycled into knives and small saws.

Using value analysis to change the material of butterfly nuts

Before improvement:
Die-cast butterfly nuts of zinc alloy were used to attach fixtures. Forty thousand nuts, each costing $.0065, were used each month (total cost: $260).

Improvement:
The nut was changed to a pressed iron piece costing $.0054 apiece.

Benefit:
Cost was reduced by $34 per month.

Improvement Example

Turning a discarded vernier caliper into a new measurement tool

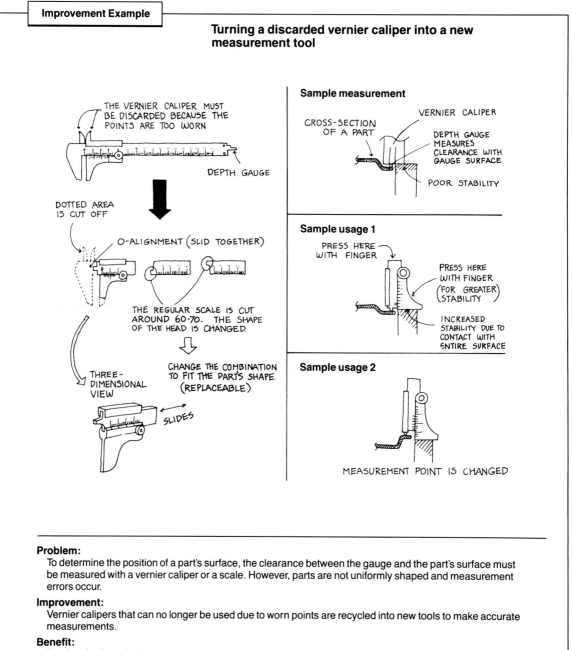

THE VERNIER CALIPER MUST BE DISCARDED BECAUSE THE POINTS ARE TOO WORN

DEPTH GAUGE

DOTTED AREA IS CUT OFF

0-ALIGNMENT (SLID TOGETHER)

THE REGULAR SCALE IS CUT AROUND 60-70. THE SHAPE OF THE HEAD IS CHANGED.

CHANGE THE COMBINATION TO FIT THE PART'S SHAPE. (REPLACEABLE)

THREE-DIMENSIONAL VIEW

SLIDES

Sample measurement

CROSS-SECTION OF A PART

VERNIER CALIPER

DEPTH GAUGE MEASURES CLEARANCE WITH GAUGE SURFACE

POOR STABILITY

Sample usage 1

PRESS HERE WITH FINGER

PRESS HERE WITH FINGER (FOR GREATER STABILITY)

INCREASED STABILITY DUE TO CONTACT WITH ENTIRE SURFACE

Sample usage 2

MEASUREMENT POINT IS CHANGED

Problem:
To determine the position of a part's surface, the clearance between the gauge and the part's surface must be measured with a vernier caliper or a scale. However, parts are not uniformly shaped and measurement errors occur.

Improvement:
Vernier calipers that can no longer be used due to worn points are recycled into new tools to make accurate measurements.

Benefit:
Previously discarded tools can be used. Because scales from vernier calipers are used, measurement errors do not occur. The tool fits the shape of the measured object and can be braced against it, giving more accurate measure.

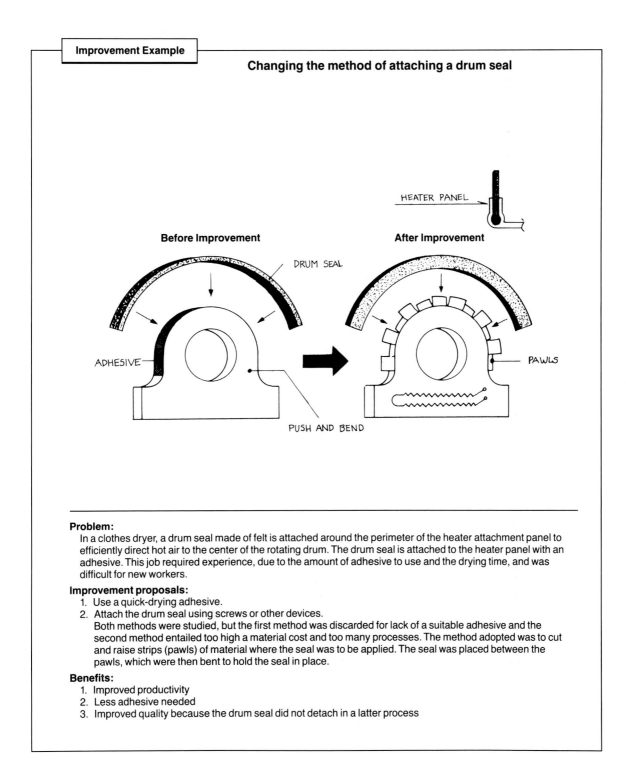

Improvement Example

Changing the method of attaching a drum seal

HEATER PANEL

Before Improvement   **After Improvement**

DRUM SEAL

ADHESIVE

PUSH AND BEND

PAWLS

Problem:
In a clothes dryer, a drum seal made of felt is attached around the perimeter of the heater attachment panel to efficiently direct hot air to the center of the rotating drum. The drum seal is attached to the heater panel with an adhesive. This job required experience, due to the amount of adhesive to use and the drying time, and was difficult for new workers.

Improvement proposals:
1. Use a quick-drying adhesive.
2. Attach the drum seal using screws or other devices.
   Both methods were studied, but the first method was discarded for lack of a suitable adhesive and the second method entailed too high a material cost and too many processes. The method adopted was to cut and raise strips (pawls) of material where the seal was to be applied. The seal was placed between the pawls, which were then bent to hold the seal in place.

Benefits:
1. Improved productivity
2. Less adhesive needed
3. Improved quality because the drum seal did not detach in a latter process

Improvement Example

Improving a product supply device with a sieve

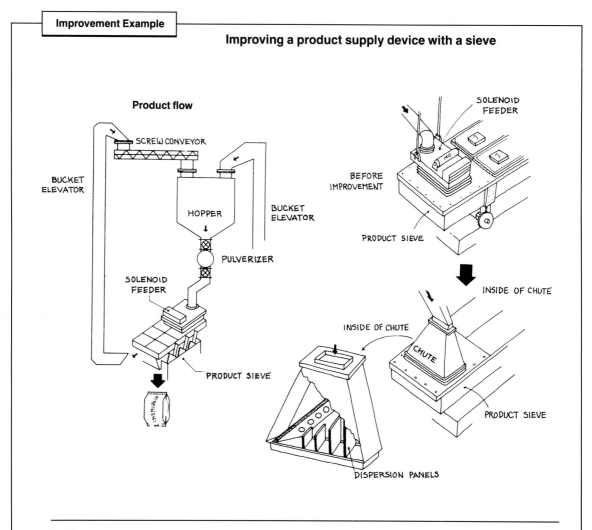

Product flow

SCREW CONVEYOR

BUCKET ELEVATOR

HOPPER

PULVERIZER

BUCKET ELEVATOR

SOLENOID FEEDER

PRODUCT SIEVE

CHEMICAL

SOLENOID FEEDER

BEFORE IMPROVEMENT

PRODUCT SIEVE

INSIDE OF CHUTE

INSIDE OF CHUTE

CHUTE

PRODUCT SIEVE

DISPERSION PANELS

Problem:
The pulverized product that emerges from the hopper is sifted by the product sieve before being packed and shipped. The solenoid feeder attached to the sieve clogs easily.

Improvement plans:
1. Steepen the angle to the feeder so that the product flows better.
2. Buff the inner surface so that the product slides better.
3. Increase the amplitude of the feeder so that clogging becomes less likely.

All three approaches were tried, but clogging occurred after two months of use in each case. Finally, the feeder was removed, the up-and-down movement of the sieve was used to disperse and supply the pulverized product, and dispersion panels were installed in the chute.

Benefits:
1. The sieving efficiency was improved and clogging no longer occurs.
2. Repair costs are saved. Electrical power is no longer needed to run the motor.

Improvements in Energy Conservation
Identifying Potential Improvements

Electrical usage

- Avoid running a motor with no load or with a very light load.
- Do not overstress bearings, gears, and other drive components of a motor.
- Operate air compressors at the proper pressure.
- Mix general and localized lighting wisely.
- Use a reasonable lighting intensity.
- Use sunlight where possible.
- Keep lighting equipment clean.
- White fluorescent lamps are 10 percent more efficient than daylight-color fluorescent lamps.

Air conditioning

- Consider using an insulation material.
- Prevent wasteful entry of outside air.
- Provide air conditioning only where necessary.

Water

- Processing and transporting water requires energy.
- Match the quality of water to its purpose.
- Consider water recycling or reprocessing.
- Prevent water leakage.
- Use brushing and other mechanical processes when cleaning; do not rely solely on water pressure.

Fuel and gas

- Use the optimum fuel in terms of price and purpose.
- Is there efficient temperature distribution in the furnace?
- How is the combustion condition?
- Is the air-to-fuel ratio correct?
- Is the proper burner being used? Is the burner maintained well?
- Is the furnace properly insulated?
- Is there a way to recover the waste heat?

Steam

- Is steam leaking?
- Is there an unnecessary surface dissipating heat?
- Is heat being conserved well?
- Is the trap working well?
- Is the type of steam being used appropriate for its purpose?
- Are the heat transfer surfaces of heat exchangers and so on kept clean?
- Is the drain being recovered?
- Can flash steam be used?

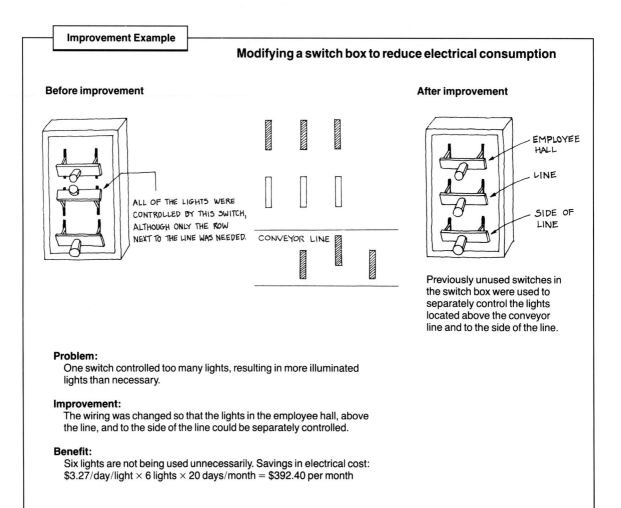

Improvement Example

Modifying a switch box to reduce electrical consumption

Before improvement

ALL OF THE LIGHTS WERE CONTROLLED BY THIS SWITCH, ALTHOUGH ONLY THE ROW NEXT TO THE LINE WAS NEEDED.

CONVEYOR LINE

After improvement

EMPLOYEE HALL

LINE

SIDE OF LINE

Previously unused switches in the switch box were used to separately control the lights located above the conveyor line and to the side of the line.

Problem:
One switch controlled too many lights, resulting in more illuminated lights than necessary.

Improvement:
The wiring was changed so that the lights in the employee hall, above the line, and to the side of the line could be separately controlled.

Benefit:
Six lights are not being used unnecessarily. Savings in electrical cost:
$3.27/day/light × 6 lights × 20 days/month = $392.40 per month

Improvement Example

Insulating a steam trap

Insulating the steam trap

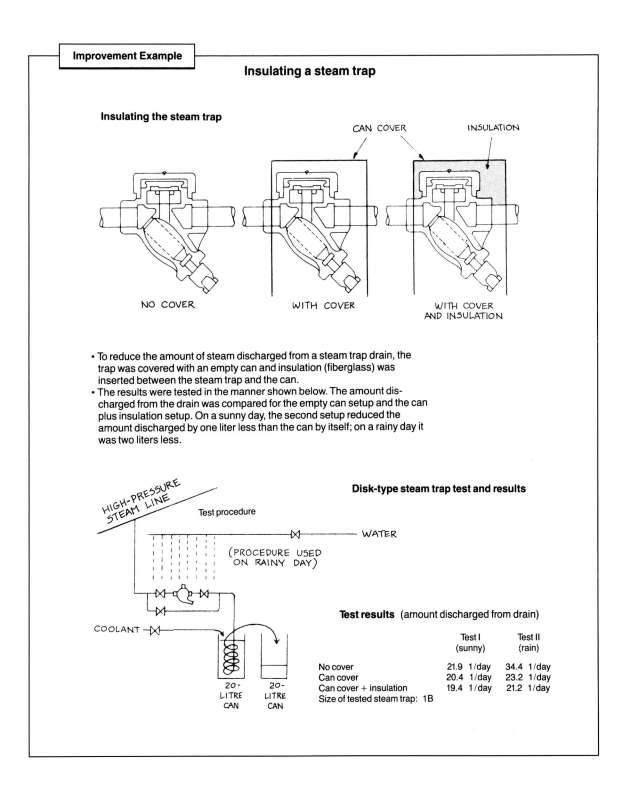

CAN COVER   INSULATION

NO COVER   WITH COVER   WITH COVER
                                 AND INSULATION

- To reduce the amount of steam discharged from a steam trap drain, the trap was covered with an empty can and insulation (fiberglass) was inserted between the steam trap and the can.
- The results were tested in the manner shown below. The amount discharged from the drain was compared for the empty can setup and the can plus insulation setup. On a sunny day, the second setup reduced the amount discharged by one liter less than the can by itself; on a rainy day it was two liters less.

HIGH-PRESSURE STEAM LINE

Test procedure

WATER

(PROCEDURE USED ON RAINY DAY)

COOLANT

20-LITRE CAN   20-LITRE CAN

Disk-type steam trap test and results

Test results (amount discharged from drain)

	Test I (sunny)	Test II (rain)
No cover	21.9 1/day	34.4 1/day
Can cover	20.4 1/day	23.2 1/day
Can cover + insulation	19.4 1/day	21.2 1/day
Size of tested steam trap: 1B		

Improvement Example

Reducing the air-blow time

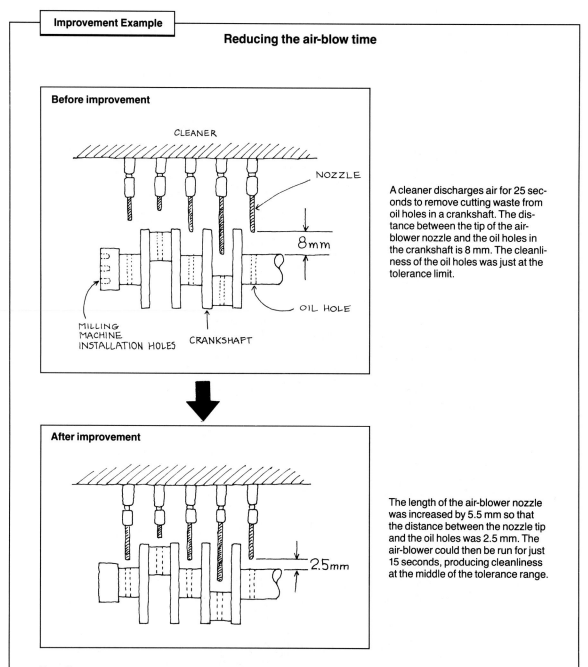

Before improvement

A cleaner discharges air for 25 seconds to remove cutting waste from oil holes in a crankshaft. The distance between the tip of the air-blower nozzle and the oil holes in the crankshaft is 8 mm. The cleanliness of the oil holes was just at the tolerance limit.

After improvement

The length of the air-blower nozzle was increased by 5.5 mm so that the distance between the nozzle tip and the oil holes was 2.5 mm. The air-blower could then be run for just 15 seconds, producing cleanliness at the middle of the tolerance range.

Benefit:
By reducing the distance between the oil holes and the nozzle tip, the air-blower effect was increased. This improved the cleanliness and reduced the air-blowing time. Savings in energy cost amounted to $642 per month.

Improvements in Clerical Work
Identifying Potential Improvements

Clerical procedure

- Is there a different way of doing the clerical work?
- Can the retrieval or the returning be done in one motion?
- Can cumbersome preparatory steps be eliminated?
- Can the task be streamlined?
- Are the tasks redundant?
- Is one worker being asked to do too much clerical work?

Forms

- Are the forms necessary?
- Can the number of forms be reduced?
- Can similar forms be consolidated into one?
- Can the number of items to be filled be reduced?
- Is it possible to write less?

Organization and orderliness

- Gather like things together.
- Is too much time being spent on looking?
- Can color-coding be used?
- Are frequently used things located near you?
- Are seldom-used things located farther away from you?
- Can something be discarded?
- Can a partition be used?

Work environment

- Is there adequate ventilation?
- Is there proper lighting?
- Can different time periods be used?
- Is the height of desks, chairs, or workbenches correct?
- Are electrical cords from machines in the way?
- Can goods be moved?
- Should the layout be changed?

Items subject to wear and tear

- Can they be recycled?
- Can they be recovered?
- Can their use be stopped?
- Can their use be reduced?
- Can the material be changed?

Improvement Example

Simple clerical task improvements

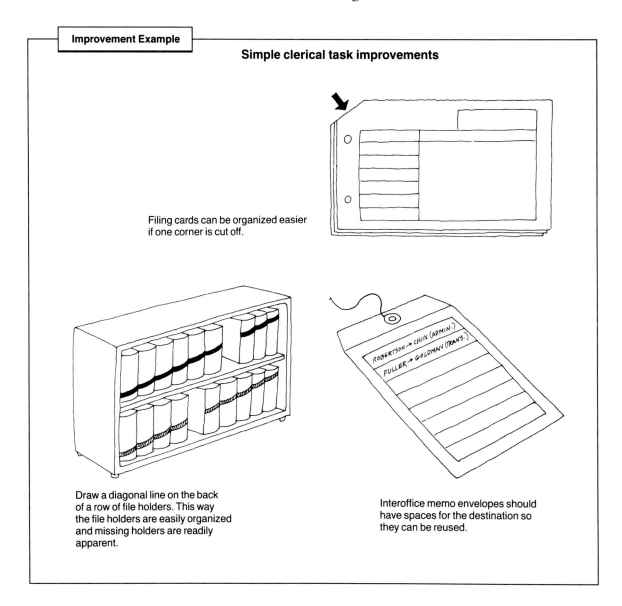

Filing cards can be organized easier if one corner is cut off.

Draw a diagonal line on the back of a row of file holders. This way the file holders are easily organized and missing holders are readily apparent.

Interoffice memo envelopes should have spaces for the destination so they can be reused.

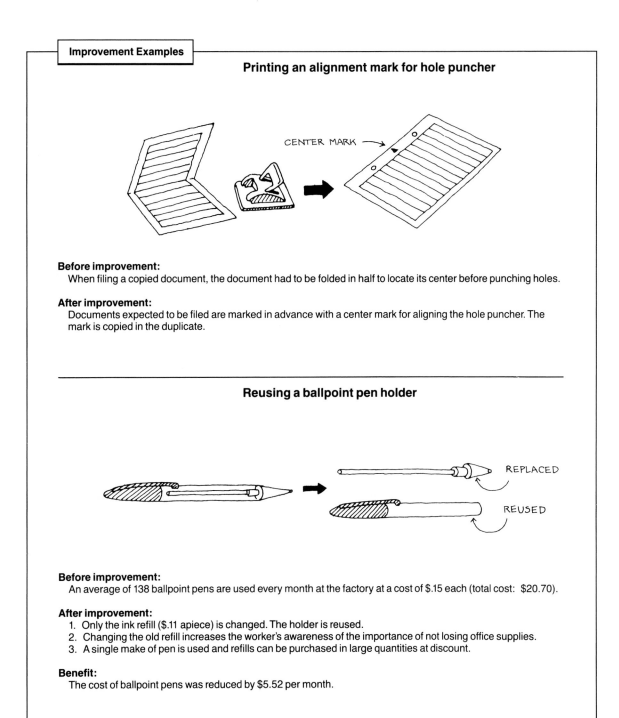

Improvement Examples

Printing an alignment mark for hole puncher

Before improvement:
When filing a copied document, the document had to be folded in half to locate its center before punching holes.

After improvement:
Documents expected to be filed are marked in advance with a center mark for aligning the hole puncher. The mark is copied in the duplicate.

Reusing a ballpoint pen holder

Before improvement:
An average of 138 ballpoint pens are used every month at the factory at a cost of $.15 each (total cost: $20.70).

After improvement:
1. Only the ink refill ($.11 apiece) is changed. The holder is reused.
2. Changing the old refill increases the worker's awareness of the importance of not losing office supplies.
3. A single make of pen is used and refills can be purchased in large quantities at discount.

Benefit:
The cost of ballpoint pens was reduced by $5.52 per month.

Improvement Example

Regulations regarding mailing of parcels and mail

Problem:

Parcels and mail were being mailed by the warehouse section. However, because the mailing procedure was not clearly established, the following problems occurred:

> 1. Forgetting to load a parcel or mail
> 2. Destination or sender not known because shipping request incomplete
> 3. Parcel or mail being shelved because not accompanied by a shipping request
> 4. Inadequate knowledge of what is to be mailed

After improvement:

The mailing procedure was clearly defined to minimize unnecessary load on the mailing section

> **Rules:**
> 1. Only business mail is accepted
> 2. The mail-request window will be located in the product warehouse office
> 3. The warehouse section must confirm that the good is mailed
> 4. When requesting to mail a good, the following information must be entered in the record book:

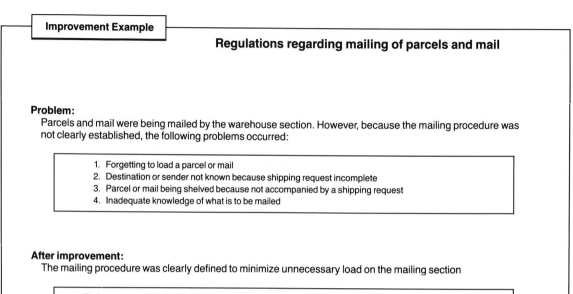

Date received	Package type and quantity	Sender	Destination	Addressee
JUNE 20	2 CARDBOARD BOXES 1 PAPER BAG	INVENTORY OFFICE	IDAHO BRANCH OFFICE	KELSO

Benefits:

> 1. What is being mailed and what is being received are now clearly known
> 2. The storage area is better organized and more orderly
> 3. When a mistake occurs, pertinent information, such as the sender and the addressee, is readily available
> 4. Reduced paperwork
> 5. Shipping errors (forgetting to mail, and the like) have been eliminated

Improvements in Sales Operations

Identifying Potential Improvements

Improving a sales operation

- Can an activity be stopped?
- Can waste be eliminated?
- Can a process be speeded up?
- Can several items be combined into one?
- Can a substitute be used?
- Can something else be used to increase efficiency?
- Can the space be used more efficiently?
- Can it be made readily obvious?
- Can communication be improved?

Improving service and trust

- Can trust be improved?
- How can you better keep promises made to customers?
- What services are attractive to customers?
- Are you making customers feel uncomfortable or risky?

Promoting sales

- How can market needs be monitored?
- How can you be the first to take advantage of a trend?
- Can merchandising methods be combined or concentrated?
- How can you distinguish the sales area from that of other stores?
- How can you build a steady customer base?

Ideas for new products

- Can dimensional or quantitative differences be used to discriminate products?
- Can products requiring less labor be used?
- Can different functions be combined to produce a synergistic effect?
- Are there new uses?
- What products will appeal to new lifestyles?

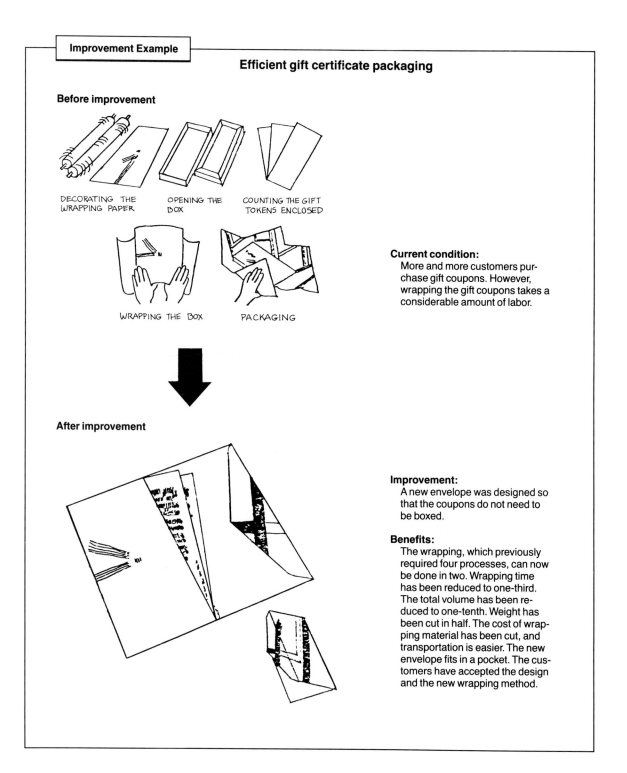

Improvement Example

Efficient gift certificate packaging

Before improvement

DECORATING THE
WRAPPING PAPER

OPENING THE
BOX

COUNTING THE GIFT
TOKENS ENCLOSED

WRAPPING THE BOX

PACKAGING

Current condition:
More and more customers purchase gift coupons. However,
wrapping the gift coupons takes a
considerable amount of labor.

After improvement

Improvement:
A new envelope was designed so
that the coupons do not need to
be boxed.

Benefits:
The wrapping, which previously
required four processes, can now
be done in two. Wrapping time
has been reduced to one-third.
The total volume has been reduced to one-tenth. Weight has
been cut in half. The cost of wrapping material has been cut, and
transportation is easier. The new
envelope fits in a pocket. The customers have accepted the design
and the new wrapping method.

Improvement Examples

Campaign to never say "I don't know"

Suggestion:

The company philosphy is for each salesperson to take good care of the customers. To implement this philosophy into good service, a campaign was begun for employees to stop saying "I don't know" and to instead say "Please wait while I get the person in charge."

Implementation:

The campaign was conducted for two months. Posters were displayed to encourage the salespeople and appropriate ways of responding to customers were taught. Employees wore an emblem below their name tags describing the campaign.

Initial-stamping bank transfer forms

Problem:

After money is transferred to a bank from a company, all questions from the bank are directed to the company's financial department. However, there was a problem in identifying the worker in the financial department who had handled the fund transfer.

Improvement:

The worker who handles a fund transfer is now required to stamp his or her initials next to the amount on the fund transfer form.

CHAPTER 9

More about Suggestion Systems

History of the Suggestion System

Meyasubako (Guideline Box)

In August 1721, a small box called the *meyasubako* was placed at the Takinoguchi entrance to Edo Castle by the order of Yoshimune Tokugawa, the eighth shogun. All citizens, regardless of their social standing, were allowed to drop written suggestions, requests, and complaints into the box. The *meyasubako* was the shogun's way of finding out how people felt about his policies and what people were thinking in general. Good suggestions were rewarded, and a man named Sensen Ogawa wrote a suggestion that led to the opening of a health-care facility (Koishigawa Yoseijo) for the poor. A suggestion dropped in the *meyasubako* also led to the development of a fire-fighting policy for the city of Edo.

As a feudal lord some twenty years earlier, Yoshimune had set up a "complaint box" by the gate to his residence, the Wakayama Castle. But in those days, making a direct appeal to the shogun was punishable by decapitation. People had to risk their lives to make suggestions to the policy makers. Yoshimune's complaint and suggestion boxes, therefore, were radically new ideas.

Written on the *meyasubako* were the words "Make your idea known. Rewards are given for ideas that are accepted." Of course, there were no established evaluation standards, and whether an idea was accepted depended on the arbitrary judgment of the administrator. However, if you look at a suggestion system as a method of soliciting opinions and ideas from the masses for making improvements, the *meyasubako* and the present-day suggestion system serve the same purpose.

Early Suggestion Systems

The practice of soliciting suggestions from workers was first used by management about 100 years ago in Scotland. William Denny, a Scottish shipbuilder, asked his workers to suggest methods for building ships at a low cost.

In the United States, records show that an Eastman Kodak employee named William Connors received a prize of two dollars in 1898 for suggesting that windows be washed to keep the workplaces brighter. Frank Lovejoy, the superior who accepted Connors' suggestion, later became the president of Kodak.

The tradition of *meyasubako* remained in Japan after Yoshimune's rule, but the number of accepted suggestions dropped dramatically. The forerunner of the modern Japanese-style suggestion system undoubtedly originated in the West. The suggestion systems of Europe and the United States had characteristics we recognize today, such as evaluating suggestions by established criteria and giving rewards not as token gifts but as the value equivalents of the ideas.

In 1905, Kanebuchi Boseki, a textile company, set up "suggestion boxes" that were reportedly an imitation of the NCR suggestion system that its management team had observed on an earlier visit to the United States. Before World War II, however, Japanese suggestion systems were generally reserved for only a handful of elite workers who had the ability and the enthusiasm to submit ideas.

Popularization Based on TWI

TWI (Training Within Industries), introduced to Japanese industry in 1949 by the U.S. occupation forces, had a major effect in expanding the suggestion system to involve all workers rather than just a handful of the elite. Job modification constituted a part of TWI and as foremen and supervisors taught workers how to perform job modification, they learned how to make changes and suggestions.

Japanese executives who traveled to the United States after the war were impressed by U.S. suggestion systems. Many Japanese companies introduced suggestion systems to follow up on the job modification movement begun by TWI. This occurred at Toshiba in 1946, at Matsushita Electric in 1950, and at Toyota in 1951. Many other companies began suggestion systems during the 1950s.

The Japanese media reported on the "blossoming suggestion systems," and suggestion boxes were set up in many offices during the 1950s. Although the suggestion system was pushed vigorously, it was still a direct copy of the Western suggestion system. A major problem in those days was getting workers to write their first suggestions.

Even though individual workers were often very talented, the workers as a group were hesitant and did not respond well to campaigns and promotional programs set up by management or by the suggestion system office. Writing itself was inconvenient for many on the production floor. Finding the time to write was another problem. Moreover, it was difficult for a worker to write a suggestion and receive a reward when all the other workers considered suggestion writing a burden and were not doing it.

In the West, where individualism is the rule, making suggestions and receiving rewards were not a problem. There was no stigma attached to selling your idea to your company. This was not the case in Japan, which is traditionally more group-oriented.

Full Participation

During the mid-1950s to the mid-1960s, most Japanese companies that had suggestion systems averaged less than one suggestion per worker per year. Those who made suggestions were considered "fanatics" by their co-workers. The workers were given opportunities to make suggestions and TWI had taught them how to make improvements. But group-oriented thinking still impeded their acceptance of the suggestion system.

The key to overcoming the final obstacle was small group activities, which shaped the suggestion system to fit the Japanese preference for group-based behavior. Group suggestion-making became a common practice in Japan.

QC circles began in Japan in 1962 as a response to the publication of a magazine called *Genba To QC* (*Quality Control for the Foreman*) by the Japan Union of Scientists and Engineers (JUSE). Around 1965, QC circle activity initiated the Zero Defects (ZD) movement, in which individual workers made a contract with their company to produce defect-free products. Spurred by the ZD movement and the QC circles, other production floor activities to improve quality and reduce errors spread like wildfire among large Japanese companies.

It was natural, therefore, for small groups to become the core units of activity in a participative suggestion system. Communication improved and supervisors and circle suggestion leaders were able to directly ask the other six or seven group members to make suggestions or to take turns serving as suggestion leaders.

Japanese suggestion activity, which stresses participation, soon became a part of other group activities. This led to the practice of groups of workers looking for problems, suggesting ideas, and then correcting the problems.

Production Floor Involvement

The group-oriented Japanese suggestion system continued to develop. The Japanese system caught up and overtook its U.S. counterpart probably in the mid-1960s when more than half of the qualified workers started making suggestions and the average number of suggestions per worker per year topped one.

The number of suggestions made by workers per year increased steadily. After the 1973 oil crisis, however, the number of suggestions accelerated geometrically. The oil crisis had forced temporary layoffs and voluntary retirements. By 1975, the initial shock of the crisis had worn off and most companies were convinced that they needed the concerted effort of the workers in order to overcome business crises.

One characteristic of the suggestion activity in those days was the importance of production floor involvement, an effect encouraged by decentralizing the suggestion system. As the number of suggestions reached one per worker per year, it became physically impossible to continue processing them centrally for the entire company. Most of the evaluation, rewarding, and clerical work were reorganized to be handled by individual management units at the plant level or even at the front-line supervisor level. This decentralization focused attention on the production floors and drew them into greater involvement.

Performing improvement activities in small groups raised the improvement knowledge and skills of production floor teams to unprecedented heights. The workers were able to experience the pleasure of not just making suggestions but actually implementing their improvement ideas, bringing the suggestion system to a new level.

The "implemented suggestions" submitted by workers might be more appropriately thought of as "improvement reports," since the idea is put into effect before it is actually suggested. The term is used, however, since even implemented

History of Modern Suggestion Systems

1898 Eastman Kodak accepts first employee suggestion.

1905 Suggestion boxes are set up in Kanebuchi Boseki.

1946 Tokyo Shibaura Denki (Toshiba) starts its "improvement suggestion system."

1949 TWI is introduced to Japan.

1950 Matsushita Electric Industrial starts its "suggestion reward system."

1951 Toyota Motor starts "creative suggestion system." Suggestion systems are begun in many other companies.

1957 Brainstorming is introduced.

1958 The Japan Federation of Employers' Associations (Nikkeiren) publishes *The Status of the Suggestion System in Japan.*

1960 The Japan HR Association conducts the first research on the suggestion system, reporting that the system is widespread but the results are poor.

1962 The QC circle movement starts (Nikka Giren).

1964 Japan HR Association survey of suggestion systems shows average of 0.3 suggestions per worker per year for 32 companies.

1965 The first ZD group starts at NEC. Rising interest in using a goal management system.

1968 Japan HR Association survey of suggestion systems shows average of 1.5 suggestions per worker per year for 60 companies.

1969 The Japan Iron and Steel Federation initiates industry-wide voluntary management activities.

1970 Japan HR Association survey shows average of 3.43 suggestions per worker per year for 60 companies.
• At Matsushita Electric, the figure exceeds 10.

1972 Japan HR Association survey shows average of 4.16 suggestions per worker per year for 54 companies.

1973 Japan HR Association survey shows average of 4.53 suggestions per worker per year for 148 companies.

1974 Japan HR Association survey shows average of 4.61 suggestions per worker per year for 153 companies.

1975 Japan HR Association survey shows average of 4.71 suggestions per worker per year for 202 companies.
• At Toshiba, more than 1.08 million suggestions were made in a year.
• Sumitomo Metal Industries averaged more than 20 suggestions per worker per year.

1976 Japan HR Association survey shows average of 5.07 suggestions per worker per year for 238 companies.

1977 Japan HR Association survey shows average of 5.58 suggestions per worker per year for 244 companies.

1978 Japan HR Association survey shows average of 8.32 suggestions per worker per year for 244 companies.
• At Matsushita Electric, more than 1.77 million suggestions were made in a year.
• Tomokazu Hori of Matsushita made over 4,000 suggestions in one year.

1979 Japan HR Association survey shows average of 7.19 suggestions per worker per year for 400 companies.
• At Hitachi, 2.29 million suggestions were made in one year.
• Fuji Electric averaged 99 suggestions per worker per year.

improvements are still subject to evaluation and rewarding based on established criteria.

The trend toward "implemented suggestion" systems has brought about a dramatic increase in the number of suggestions. In companies with several hundred thousand suggestions annually, more than half of these are "implemented suggestions." With the emergence of "implemented suggestion" systems, suggestion activity is becoming one with improvement activity.

Suggestion Systems in Management
The Suggestion System as a Motivational Tool

The most important concern of the person at the top of any hierarchical organization is how to get workers to use their full potential. Since the nineteenth century, students of management and behavioral science have searched for ways to manage and motivate workers for higher productivity. It is now known that standardization of tasks is effective and that workers cannot be motivated by verbal or physical threats. Workers do display unexpected ability, however, when they find meaning in their work. This meaning is not something they can be told to find; they have to find it themselves.

These things have been known a long time. The question is, how can this well-understood principle be put into actual practice in managing a company? The postwar history of voluntary improvement activities in Japan is one story of the search for the answer.

One secret of Japan's industrial success is that the activity unit was reduced to the small group, allowing closer communication. Another reason is that the results of small-group activities were expressed as "suggestions." Workers previously isolated in performing monotonous mechanical labor found camaraderie in small groups. They learned the joy of creating in cooperation with fellow group members. Moreover, their activities produce tangible results. Seeing the difference they can make brings great satisfaction to the workers and working becomes a more pleasant experience.

The Suggestion System as an Employee Development Tool

The modern improvement suggestion system can be summarized as a management system to elicit the self-motivation of the workers. Workers become self-motivated when they realize that their voluntary activity is indispensable to management and a vital element in the company's success.

Making the workers realize this, however, requires the support of top management, supervisors, and members of the suggestion office staff. The importance of this support has been emphasized throughout this handbook, but we will say it one more time. Without the support of top management, supervisors, and suggestion office staff, voluntary suggestion activity will not succeed. A successful suggestion system will enhance communication, improve camaraderie in the workplace, and invigorate the organization. It is definitely worth the commitment it requires.

The annual economic benefits of the suggestion system in Japan are estimated at ¥100 to ¥200 billion ($436,700 to $873,400). This savings nevertheless represents only a small fraction of all efforts expended by companies to cut costs. The suggestion system would be too indirect a tool if its sole purpose were to cut costs. If evaluated only in terms of its cost-cutting potential, a suggestion system would probably be too wasteful. Each suggestion must be meticulously written, examined, rewarded, and managed. Suggestion campaigns and other festivities are periodically necessary, requiring some expense to carry out.

The true value of a suggestion system, however, is as a tool for encouraging each worker to consider his or her job in a progressive light, to understand where he or she fits into the entire corporate structure, and to grow as a member of the corporation. Taken in this context, readers will realize that the suggestion system is actually an excellent tool for improving morale, developing human resources, and invigorating a company. It is valuable because it is voluntary, and its success depends on the participation and support of all employees.

Effects of a Participatory Suggestion System

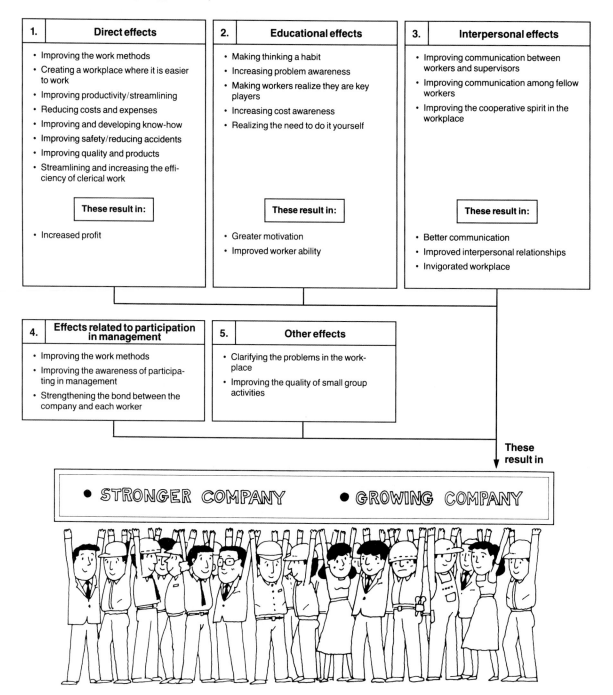

1.	**Direct effects**

- Improving the work methods
- Creating a workplace where it is easier to work
- Improving productivity/streamlining
- Reducing costs and expenses
- Improving and developing know-how
- Improving safety/reducing accidents
- Improving quality and products
- Streamlining and increasing the efficiency of clerical work

These result in:

- Increased profit

2.	**Educational effects**

- Making thinking a habit
- Increasing problem awareness
- Making workers realize they are key players
- Increasing cost awareness
- Realizing the need to do it yourself

These result in:

- Greater motivation
- Improved worker ability

3.	**Interpersonal effects**

- Improving communication between workers and supervisors
- Improving communication among fellow workers
- Improving the cooperative spirit in the workplace

These result in:

- Better communication
- Improved interpersonal relationships
- Invigorated workplace

4.	**Effects related to participation in management**

- Improving the work methods
- Improving the awareness of participating in management
- Strengthening the bond between the company and each worker

5.	**Other effects**

- Clarifying the problems in the workplace
- Improving the quality of small group activities

These result in

- STRONGER COMPANY   • GROWING COMPANY

Index

Books Available
from Productivity Press

Productivity Press publishes and distributes materials on productivity, quality improvement, and employee involvement for business and industry, academia, and the general market. Many products are direct source materials from Japan that have been translated into English for the first time and are available exclusively from Productivity. Supplemental services include conferences, seminars, in-house training programs, and industrial study missions. Send for free book catalog.

Canon Production System
Creative Involvement of the Total Workforce
compiled by the Japan Management Association

A fantastic success story! Canon set a goal to increase productivity by three percent per month — and achieved it! The first book-length case study to show how to combine the most effective Japanese management principles and quality improvement techniques into one overall strategy that improves every area of the company on a continual basis.
ISBN 0-915299-06-2 / 232 pages / $36.95

Introduction to TPM
Total Productive Maintenance
by Seiichi Nakajima

Total Productive Maintenance (TPM) combines the American practice of preventive maintenance with the Japanese concept of total quality control and total employee involvement. The result is an innovative system for equipment maintenance that optimizes effectiveness, eliminates breakdowns, and promotes autonomous operator maintenance through day-to-day activities. This book summarizes the steps involved in TPM and provides case examples from several Japanese plants.
ISBN 0-915299-23-2 / 168 pages / $39.95

TPM Development Program
Implementing Total Productive Maintenance
by Seiichi Nakajima

This book outlines a three-year program for systematic TPM development and implementation. It describes in detail the five principal developmental activities of TPM:

1. Systematic elimination of the six big equipment related losses through small group activities
2. Autonomous maintenance (by operators)
3. Scheduled maintenance for the maintenance department
4. Training in operation and maintenance skills
5. Comprehensive equipment management from the design stage

ISBN 0-915299-37-2 / 352 pages / $65.00

Productivity Press, Inc., Dept. BK, P.O. Box 3007, Cambridge, MA 02140 1-800-274-9911

Zero Quality Control
Source Inspection and the Poka-Yoke System
by Shigeo Shingo, translated by Andrew P. Dillon

This book demonstrates how source inspection (detecting errors before they become defects) can eliminate the need for statistical quality control. It goes into the nitty-gritty of Poka-yoke and ZQC and shows how to turn out the highest quality products in the shortest period of time.
ISBN 0-915299-07-0 / 305 pages / $65.00

Poka-Yoke
Improving Product Quality by Preventing Defects
compiled by Nikkan Kogyo Shimbun, Ltd./Factory Magazine (ed.)
preface by Shigeo Shingo

If your goal is 100% zero defects, here is the book for you — a completely illustrated guide to poka-yoke (mistake-proofing) for supervisors and shop-floor workers. Many poka-yoke devices come from line workers and are implemented with the help of engineering staff. The result is better product quality — and greater participation by workers in efforts to improve your processes, your products, and your company as a whole.
ISBN 0-915299-31-1 / 288 pages / $59.95

Managerial Engineering
Techniques for Improving Quality and
Productivity in the Workplace
by Ryuji Fukuda

A proven path to managerial success, based on reliable methods developed by one of Japan's leading productivity experts and winner of the prestigious Deming prize. Dr. W. Edwards Deming, world-famous consultant in statistical studies, says of the book, "Provides an excellent and clear description of the devotion and methods of Japanese management to continual improvement of quality, knowing well that as efforts succeed in improvement of quality, productivity improves, costs go down."
ISBN 0-915299-09-7 / 179 pages / $34.95

Productivity Press, Inc., Dept. BK, P.O. Box 3007, Cambridge, MA 02140 1-800-274-9911

BOOKS AVAILABLE FROM PRODUCTIVITY PRESS

Christopher, William F. **Productivity Measurement Handbook**
ISBN 0-915299-05-4 / 1983 / 680 pages / looseleaf / $137.95

Ford, Henry. **Today and Tomorrow** (originally published 1926)
ISBN 0-915299-36-4 / 1988 / 302 pages / hardcover / $24.95

Fukuda, Ryuji. **Managerial Engineering: Techniques for Improving Quality and Productivity in the Workplace**
ISBN 0-915299-09-7 / 1984 / 206 pages / hardcover / $34.95

Hatakeyama, Yoshio. **Manager Revolution! A Guide to Survival in Today's Changing Workplace**
ISBN 0-915299-10-0 / 1984 / 198 pages / hardcover / $24.95

Japan Human Resources Association. **The Idea Book: Improvement Through Total Employee Involvement**
ISBN 0-915299-22-4 / 1988 / 218 pages / $49.95

Japan Management Association and Constance E. Dyer.
Canon Production System: Creative Involvement of the Total Workforce
ISBN 0-915299-06-2 / 1987 / 251 pages / hardcover / $36.95

Japan Management Association. **Kanban and Just-In-Time at Toyota: Management Begins at the Workplace, Revised Edition,** translated by David J. Lu
ISBN 0-915299-08-9 / 1986 / 224 pages / hardcover / $29.95

Karatsu, Hajime. **Tough Words for American Industry**
ISBN 0-915299-25-9 / 1988 / 179 pages / hardcover / $24.95

Karatsu, Hajime. **TQC Wisdom of Japan: Managing for Total Quality Control**
ISBN 0-915299-18-6 / 1988 / 138 pages / hardcover / $29.95

Lu, David J. **Inside Corporate Japan: The Art of Fumble-Free Management**
ISBN 0-915299-16-X / 1987 / 278 pages / hardcover / $24.95

Mizuno, Shigeru (ed.) **Management for Quality Improvement: The 7 New QC Tools**
ISBN 0-915299-29-1 / 1988 / 326 pages / hardcover / $59.95

Nakajima, Seiichi. **Introduction to Total Productive Maintenance**
ISBN 0-915299-23-2 / 1988 / 129 pages / $39.95

Nikkan Kogyo Shimbun. **Poka-yoke: Improving Product Quality by Preventing Defects**
ISBN 0-915299-31-3 / 1988 / 288 pages / $49.95

Ohno, Taiichi. **Toyota Production System: Beyond Large-Scale Production**
ISBN 0-915299-14-3 / 1988 / 176 pages / hardcover / $39.95

Ohno, Taiichi. **Workplace Management**
ISBN 0-915299-19-4 / 1988 / 176 pages / hardcover / $34.95

Ohno, Taiichi and Setsuo Mito. **Just-In-Time for Today and Tomorrow: A Total Management System**
ISBN 0-915299-20-8 / 1988 / 176 pages / hardcover / $34.95

Productivity Press, Inc., Dept. BK, P.O. Box 3007, Cambridge, MA 02140 1-800-274-9911

Shingo, Shigeo. **Non-Stock Production: The Shingo System for Continuous Improvement**
ISBN 0-915299-30-5 / 1988 / 480 pages / hardcover / $75.00

Shingo, Shigeo. **A Revolution in Manufacturing: The SMED System,** translated by Andrew P. Dillon
ISBN 0-915299-03-8 / 1985 / 383 pages / hardcover / $65.00

Shingo, Shigeo. **Zero Quality Control: Source Inspection and the Poka-yoke System,** translated by Andrew P. Dillon
ISBN 0-915299-07-0 / 1986 / 328 pages / hardcover / $65.00

Shingo, Shigeo. **The Sayings of Shigeo Shingo: Key Strategies for Plant Improvement,** translated by Andrew P. Dillon
ISBN 0-915299-15-1 / 1987 / 207 pages / hardcover / $36.95

Shinohara, Isao (ed.) **New Production System: JIT Crossing Industry Boundaries**
ISBN 0-915299-21-6 / 1988 / 218 pages / hardcover / $34.95

AUDIO-VISUAL PROGRAMS

Shingo, Shigeo. **The SMED System,** translated by Andrew P. Dillon
ISBN 0-915299-11-9 / 181 slides / 40 minutes / $749.00
ISBN 0-915299-27-5 / 2 videos / 40 minutes / $749.00

Shingo, Shigeo, **The Poka-yoke System**, translated by Andrew P. Dillon
ISBN 0-915299-13-5 / 224 slides / 45 minutes / $749.00
ISBN 0-915299-28-3 / 2 videos / 45 minutes / $749.00

TO ORDER: Write, phone or fax Productivity Press, Dept. BK, P.O. Box 3007, Cambridge, MA 02140, phone 617/497-5146, fax 617/868-3524. Send check or charge to your credit card (American Express, Visa, MasterCard accepted).

U.S. ORDERS: Add $3 shipping for first book, $1 each additional. CT residents add 7.5% and MA residents 5% sales tax.

FOREIGN ORDERS: Payment must be made in U.S. dollars. For Canadian orders, add $8 shipping for first book, $1 each additional. Orders to other countries are on a proforma basis; please indicate shipping method desired.

NOTE: Prices subject to change without notice.

Productivity Press, Inc., Dept. BK, P.O. Box 3007, Cambridge, MA 02140 1-800-274-9911

UTAH STATE UNIVERSITY PARTNERS PROGRAM

announces the

Shigeo Shingo Prizes for Manufacturing Excellence

for North American Businesses, Students and Faculty

ELIGIBILITY

Businesses: Applications are due in late January. They should detail the quality and productivity improvements achieved through Shingo's manufacturing methods and similar techniques. Letters of intent are required by mid-November of the previous year.

Students: Applicants from accredited schools must apply by letter before November 15 indicating what research is planned. Papers must be received by early March.

Faculty: Applicants from accredited schools must apply by letter before November 15, indicating the scope of papers planned, and submit papers by the following March.

CRITERIA

Businesses: Quality and productivity improvements achieved by using Shingo's Scientific Thinking Mechanism (STM) and his methods, such as Single-Minute-Exchange-of-Die (SMED), Poka-yoke (defect prevention), Just-In-Time (JIT), and Non-Stock Production (NSP), or similar techniques.

Students: Creative research on quality and productivity improvements through the use and extension of Shingo's STM and his manufacturing methods: SMED, NSP, and Poka-yoke.

Faculty: Papers publishable in professional journals based on empirical, conceptual or theoretical applications and extensions of Shingo's manufacturing methods for quality and productivity improvements: SMED, Poka-yoke, JIT, and NSP.

PRIZES

Awards will be presented by Shigeo Shingo at Utah State University's Partners Productivity Seminar, held in April in Logan, Utah.

Five graduate and five undergraduate student awards of $2,000, $1,500, and $1,000 to first, second, and third place winners, respectively, and $500 to fourth and fifth place winners.

Three faculty awards of $3,000, $2,000 and $1,000, respectively.

Six Shigeo Shingo Medallions to the top three large and small business winners.

SHINGO PRIZE COMMITTEE

Committee members representing prestigious business, professional, academic and governmental organizations worldwide will evaluate the applications and select winners, assisted by a technical examining board.

Application forms and contest information may be obtained from the Shingo Prize Committee, College of Business, UMC 3521, Utah State University, Logan, UT, 84322, 801-750-2281. All English language books by Dr. Shingo can be purchased from the publisher, Productivity Press, P.O. Box 3007, Cambridge, MA 02140: call 1-800-274-9911 or 617-497-5146.

Japan's "Dean of Quality Consultants"

SHIGEO SHINGO

Dr. Shigeo Shingo is, quite simply, the world's leading expert on improving the manufacturing process. Known as "Dr. Improvement" in Japan, he is the originator of the Single-Minute Exchange of Die (SMED) concept and the Poka-yoke defect prevention system and one of the developers of the Just-In-Time production system that helped make Toyota the most productive automobile manufacturer in the world. His work now helps hundreds of other companies worldwide save billions of dollars in manufacturing costs annually.

The most sought-after consultant in Japan, Dr. Shingo has trained more than 10,000 people in 100 companies. He established and is President of Japan's highly-regarded Institute of Management Improvement and is the author of numerous books, including *Revolution in Manufacturing: The SMED System* and *Zero Quality Control: Source Inspection and the Poka-yoke System*. His newest book, *Non-Stock Production*, concentrates on expanding U.S. manufacturers' understanding of stockless production.

Dr. Shingo's genius is his understanding of exactly why products are manufactured the way they are, and then transforming that understanding into a workable system for low-cost, high-quality production. In the history of international manufacturing, Shingo stands alongside such pioneers as Robert Fulton, Henry Ford, Frederick Taylor, and Douglas McGregor as one of the key figures in the quest for improvement.

His world-famous SMED system is known as "The Heart of Just-In-Time Manufacturing" for (1) reducing set-up time from hours to minutes; (2) cutting lead time from months to days; (3) slashing work-in-progress inventory by up to 90%; (4) involving employees in team problem solving; (5) 99% improvement in quality; and (6) 70% reduction in floor space.

Shigeo Shingo has been called the father of the second great revolution in manufacturing.
— *Quality Control Digest*

The money-saving, profit-making ideas… set forth by Shingo could do much to help U.S. manufacturers reduce set-up time, improve quality and boost productivity… all for very little cash.

— *Tooling & Production Magazine*

When Americans think about quality today, they often think of Japan. But when the Japanese think of quality, they are likely to think of Shigeo Shingo, … architect of Toyota's now famous production system.

— *Boardroom Report*

Shingo's visit to our plant was significant in making breakthroughs in productivity we previously thought impossible. The benefits… are more far-reaching than I ever anticipated.

— Gifford M. Brown, Plant Mgr.
Ford Motor Company